JEREMY FRANK & JIM PASSON JR.

Hidden Ball Trick

The Baseball Stats You Never Thought to Look For:
1876-1919 (Vol. 1)

First edition

ISBN: 9781793996930

Editing by Jon Becker

This book was professionally typeset on Reedsy.
Find out more at reedsy.com

Contents

Preface

Since the first Major League in 1876 (or 1871, depending on who you ask), the game of baseball has gone through many changes. With data going back until then, the game contains a myriad of statistical oddities, firsts, and lasts. When we first began writing this book in December of 2018, we envisioned one singular book with every year in baseball history covered. However, we got so deep into the statistics that we decided that limiting ourselves to one book would be unfair to you, the reader. Instead, we made the decision to split baseball's history up into thirds, going from 1871 (the founding of the National Association) to 1919 (the end of the Dead Ball Era) in our first volume; that's the one you're reading right now. Our second installment, which we hope to have released around the conclusion of the 2019 season, goes from the beginning of the Live Ball Era in 1920 to 1969, the year after they lowered the mound. We didn't want to cut the book off in the middle of the decade at 1968, so we added '69 for good measure. The final installment of the three will be released in the offseason following the 2019 season, with the new stats updated to include that season. This lets us finish off the 2010s instead of leaving it after 2018. That means that the first two books are updated through the 2018 baseball season, while the third is updated through 2019. While it may be a little bit annoying to someone who would need to get all three, trust us, the quality of the content inside each book is greatly enhanced thanks to this decision. We've essentially doubled the amount of statistics we have included since we didn't have to be as mindful about the rising page count.

While we both got our "starts" on Twitter, most of the stats you'll read about have not been posted by us, or anywhere else before. There's virtually an entire Twitter account's worth of tweets stored inside the three books just waiting to be read. If you haven't visited our pages, they're on the back of the book; we post any interesting baseball stats we come across. We hope you enjoy the content we've spent hours upon hours researching and putting into words, and learn as much reading it as we did writing it. We'd greatly appreciate if you spread the word to your baseball loving friends and family!

Acknowledgement

Jeremy Frank would like to thank his parents, Missy and Nolan, and his sister Allison for not only supporting him throughout the process of this book but also his entire life. Everything he's done so far in his life (at least all of the meaningful things) can be attributed to them and the encouragement and confidence they give him on a daily basis. His mom and dad got him into baseball at a young age, either coaching his little league teams or cheering said teams on very, very loudly from the stands (they know who did which). Allison went to way more games than she wanted to, and although she didn't have much of a choice, just being there meant a lot. Not only did his parents help develop Jeremy's interest in baseball, they also taught him the value of education, which is the most important thing he's learned in his life. He's grateful that they're sending him to college and that they believe in his future more than anyone else. In addition, Jeremy wants to thank Jeff Rosenberg, Dan Wolf and Wayne Silverman for helping him work out a few things along the way that helped get this book out, and the rest of his extended family for being supportive of him throughout everything he's done. Jeremy thanks his friends, specifically Adam Offenbach (who he's been best friends with since kindergarten), Brandon Ward, Josh Ezrol, and Devan Fink, for letting him ramble on about anything and everything, because he really likes to talk a lot. Sometimes they even talk a little bit about baseball. He wants to thank his teachers, for which there have been too many great ones to name. They know who they are. Lastly, Jeremy would like to thank all of his friends he has made on Twitter. It sounds kind of dumb, but many have been with him for nearly a quarter of his life, since he was 14. Despite what you may read, the Internet can be a very great place sometimes.

Jim Passon Jr., first and foremost, would like to thank his wife, Amber Passon. She sacrificed so much of their time together to make this dream of writing a series of books a reality for Jim, always encouraging him to get back on the computer after a long day at work or a tough time at the gym. Jim would also love to credit his immediate family for always supporting his love for the game of baseball. His father, Jim Sr., always took time to play catch, drag him to little league practices and games, teach him how to play and how to hustle, they collected baseball cards together, and so much more. To this day Jim Jr., Amber, and Jim Sr. make it a point to catch the Yankees series every time they are in Seattle. His mother, Marilyn, consistently made it possible for Jim to be around the game of baseball, booking trips to the Kingdome and the Metrodome for their tight-budgeted Montana family. He'll always remember how hard she worked to get those autographs from ballplayers on the Great Falls Dodgers teams as a birthday present for him. Last, but definitely not least, Jim would like to thank his sister, Jenny. No sibling could ever ask for more than she delivered. Jenny passed up many an opportunity to be involved in school activities to make sure that her brother could afford to be around the game that he loved, all while she cheered from the stands relentlessly.

Now we're in first person, writing this part together, fittingly thanking our editor/fact-checker Jon Becker. It's not often you

viii

can get an editor as versatile as Jon was for us, but his writing and baseball knowledge helped make this book look a lot better than it did after its first draft. Jon currently attends Miami University in Oxford, Ohio, and does a lot of great baseball work. You can direct any concerns regarding grammatical mistakes to Jon. We also want to thank Yunsik Jeong, our cover designer for all three volumes. He'll be attending Northwestern University in 2019 and he taught himself graphic design, which is pretty cool.

And of course, this book would not be possible without Baseball Reference's incredible Play Index tool. Most of the stats included in this book would be much more difficult to find without Baseball Reference, and it is one of the best websites on the Internet. In addition, Fangraphs, Baseball Almanac, the Society for American Baseball Research (SABR), the Baseball Hall of Fame, and the *Washington Post* were fantastic resources to us. All images you'll see in this book are in the public domain and were retrieved from the Wikimedia Commons. Lastly, thank you to Evan Boyd for helping with a few notes.

Glossary of Terms

- **Hits:** A hit is given to a player who puts the ball into play and reaches base safely without any errors or fielder's choices made. Singles, doubles, triples, and home runs are all hits.
- **Total bases:** Sort of like hits, but increases depending on the type of hit. A single is one total base, a double is two, a triple is three, and a home run is four. Walks are not included in total bases.
- **Runs batted in:** A stat meant to credit a batter for driving in a run. If there is a runner on third base and the hitter singles, they get credit for 1 RBI. Runs batted in became an official statistic in 1920, so all RBI figures from before then have been retroactively computed by historians.
- **Batting average (also BA):** Percentage of at bats resulting in a hit.
- **On-base percentage (also OBP):** Percentage of plate appearances (with a couple exceptions) in which a hitter reaches base via hit, walk, or hit by pitch.
- **Slugging percentage (also SLG):** Rate of total bases per at bat.
- **On base plus slugging (also OPS):** OBP plus SLG.

- **Triple slash line (also just slash line):** Includes BA, OBP, and SLG. A player who "slashed" .300/.400/.500 means that player had a .300 batting average, .400 on-base percentage, and .500 slugging percentage.
- **Adjusted on base plus slugging (also OPS+):** OPS+ attempts to adjust OPS for external factors such as ballpark and era. OPS+ is set to a scale of 100, so a mark of 150 means that the hitter was 50% better than the league average hitter. An example of OPS+ adjusting for era and ballpark unlike other statistics: Todd Helton had a 1.162 OPS in 2000, and Ty Cobb had an .848 OPS in 1908. At first glance, Helton's season blew Cobb's out of the water, but OPS doesn't take anything other than raw numbers into account. Helton played at Coors Field, the most hitter friendly ballpark in baseball, during a time when league-wide offensive performance was at its peak. Cobb's .848 OPS came when teams averaged 3.38 runs per game, the lowest mark ever in a season. OPS+ gives Helton a 163 for his 2003 season, which, while spectacular, falls just short of Cobb's 170. OPS+ would argue that Cobb's season was better from a hitting perspective once adjusted for the difference in run environments that the two players were forced to play in.
- **Isolated Power (also ISO):** Rate of extra bases per at bat. The equation is SLG - BA = ISO or $(2B + 2*3B + 3*HR) / AB = ISO$
- **Innings pitched (also IP):** Number of outs recorded by a pitcher divided by 3. A pitcher with 18.0 innings got 54 outs, while 18.1 innings is 55 outs (the decimal represents the remainder, as the pitcher pitched 18 and one third of an inning).
- **Batters faced (also BF):** Every batter that a pitcher faces.

2

- **Earned runs (also ER):** Runs scored not as a result of an error in the field.
- **Strikeout percentage/rate (also K%):** Percentage of plate appearances or batters faced ending in a strikeout. This stat is for both pitchers and hitters.
- **Strikeouts per nine innings pitched (also K/9):** Average amount of strikeouts by a pitcher per 9 innings pitched.
- **Walk percentage/rate (also BB%):** Strikeout percentage, but with walks instead of strikeouts.
- **Walk per nine innings pitched (also BB/9):** K/9, but with walks instead of strikeouts.
- **Earned run average (also ERA):** Average amount of earned runs allowed per 9 innings pitched.
- **Fielding independent pitching (also FIP):** A pitcher's expected ERA given four factors: strikeouts, walks, home runs allowed, and innings pitched. While ERA could be influenced by poor or great fielders, FIP is not influenced by a pitcher's defense at all and only looks at things that a pitcher is accountable for.
- **Walks and hits per inning pitched (also WHIP):** Pretty self explanatory, to be honest. Hit batsmen are not included, for some reason.
- **Win-Loss% (also W-L%):** Percentage of decisions (wins and losses) resulting in a win for a pitcher or team
- **Adjusted earned run average (also ERA+):** ERA+ is like OPS+ for pitchers, using a base stat of ERA. 100 is average, and higher is better. ERA+ looks at era (as in the time period, not the stat) and ballpark to determine just how impressive a pitcher was at preventing runs given what he had to work with.
- **Wins Above Replacement (also WAR):** Wins Above Re-

placement is seen as the quintessential advanced stat, mostly because it is the most popular. WAR attempts to combine all of a player's contributions into one number. For position players, WAR takes into account not only performance on offense, but also defense, baserunning, how important of a position one plays, era, and ballpark. For pitching, it looks at run prevention, opponent quality, era, and ballpark, among others. WAR looks at how "valuable" a player is by comparing him to a readily available replacement player. A player being worth 10 WAR simply means that if that player was replaced with a fringe Major Leaguer, his team would be expected to lose 10 more games. We won't get into all of the calculations that go into WAR right now, but you can Google it and you'll find everything that goes into it. For this book, we used Baseball Reference's version of WAR.

- **Offensive WAR (also oWAR):** Think WAR, but without defense. oWAR looks at how valuable a player is on offense given their hitting and baserunning along with what is expected at their position and taking into account ballpark and era. For example, a shortstop with the same hitting and baserunning stats as a first baseman will have a higher oWAR because it is generally more difficult to find offensive production from a shortstop than a first baseman.
- **Defensive WAR (also dWAR):** WAR, but without offense. dWAR is more accurate in recent years due to better defensive metrics, but is still around for earlier years. It also takes into account position. An elite defensive catcher will have a higher dWAR than an elite defensive first baseman.
- **National Association (also NA):** The National Association is considered by some to be the first professional baseball league. The league existed from 1871 through 1875.

- **National League (also NL):** The National League, also known as the senior circuit, is widely considered to be the first professional baseball league. The league was established in 1876 and still exists today.
- **American Association (also AA):** The American Association was a professional baseball league that was established in 1882 as a rival league to the National League. The league would be around for a decade before its final season was played in 1891.
- **Union Association (also UA):** The Union Association was a professional baseball league that did not succeed in competing against the National League and the American Association. The UA lasted just one season in 1884.
- **Players League (also PL):** The Players League, much like the UA of six years earlier, was a professional baseball league that did not succeed in competing against the National League and the American Association. The PL lasted just one season in 1890.
- **American League (also AL):** The American League, also known as the junior circuit, was established in 1901 as a rival league to the National League. The AL still remains today as the rival league to the NL. The champions of the two leagues face each other in the World Series.
- **Federal League (also FL):** The Federal League was a professional baseball league that was established in 1914. The FL lasted just two seasons in its failed attempt to compete against the powerful National and American Leagues.

The National Association (1871-1875)

The National Association of Professional Base Ball Players, started in 1871, is considered by some to be the first professional baseball league. We chose not to delve too deep into the National Association years, or any of its stats, and began with the founding of the National League in 1876. However, we did choose some of the most interesting stats from the NA's five years:

- In 1871, the Philadelphia Athletics went 21-7 and averaged a league leading 13.4 runs per game. All ten of their regular players averaged more than a run scored per game, including their pitcher/manager Dick McBride.
- In a June game in 1871, Philadelphia took on the Troy Haymakers, and chaos ensued. The Athletics won the game 49-33 in 3 hours and 55 minutes. The teams combined for 82 runs, 74 hits, and 20 errors, and the A's only left four runners on base in the entire game! The Haymakers proceeded to win their next game by a score of 37-16 over the New York Mutuals.
- Levi Meyerle led the NA with a .492 average, .500 on-base percentage, and .700 slugging percentage in the NA's first season. He went 64-for-130, a hit short of batting .500.
- Cap Anson, who made his debut as a 19-year-old for the Rockford Forest Citys, went on to have quite a career. Including his five NA seasons, Anson would post an OPS+ of

120 or better in each of his first 22 seasons, and an OPS+ of 90 or better in all 27 years of his career. He led the NA with a .455 OBP in 1872.

- Lip Pike's seven home runs in 1872 for the Baltimore Canaries were the most in a season during the five years that the National Association was in existence. Pike accounted for nearly 19% of the home runs hit in 1872 and his sixteen home runs from 1871 to 1875 were the most in the league. Does that make him the Babe Ruth of the National Association?

- In 1872, a 16-year-old named Jim Britt produced 41 hits at the plate for the Brooklyn Atlantics; at no other time in baseball history has a player that young recorded that many hits in a season. Oh, by the way, Britt threw complete games for all 37 of his team's contests that season.

- Ross Barnes batted at least .400 in each of the NA's first three seasons, slashing .424/.457/.597 through 1873. Barnes led the 1873 season in runs, hits, doubles, triples, stolen bases, walks, and all three slash stats.

- 1n 1875, Candy Cummings and Tommy Bond of the Hartford Dark Blues struck out 82 and 70 hitters, respectively. They are the only set of teammates to record 35+ strikeouts in the same NA season.

- Bobby Mathews struck out 329 hitters during the five seasons he played in the National Association, the most of any pitcher. The New York Mutuals' pitchers recorded 326 strikeouts during the team's five seasons in the NA, the most of any franchise. Mathews finished with more strikeouts in the National Association than any individual franchise, and is responsible for 18.8% of the strikeouts ever thrown in the league! If someone accounted for 18.8% of the strikeouts in 2018, that'd be a grand total of 7,747 strikeouts... for one

pitcher!
- Most hits in a season, 1871 to 1875:

```
143 - Ross Barnes (1875 Boston Red Stockings)
138 - Ross Barnes (1873 Boston Red Stockings)
138 - Cal McVey (1875 Boston Red Stockings)
136 - Deacon White (1875 Boston Red Stockings)
136 - George Wright (1875 Boston Red Stockings)
127 - Andy Leonard (1875 Boston Red Stockings)
125 - George Wright (1873 Boston Red Stockings)
123 - Cal McVey (1874 Boston Red Stockings)
122 - Deacon White (1873 Boston Red Stockings)
120 - Davy Force (1875 Philadelphia Athletics)
```

- Al Spalding led the National Association in wins in each of the Association's five seasons. He went 204-53, good for a .794 winning percentage in those years.
- While the Philadelphia Athletics took the Pennant in 1871, the Boston Red Stockings took it in each of the other four seasons.

The other stats you'll see in the rest of the book use Major League Baseball's beginning as 1876, not 1871. If a player is noted as the first player in MLB history to do something, that means he was the first since 1876 to do so.

1876

Following the folding of the National Association of Professional Base Ball Players (NA), Chicago White Stockings owner William Hulbert founded The National League of Professional Base Ball Clubs, or the NL for short. While some claim the National Association should be considered the first major league, most historians point towards 1876 and the National League's creation as baseball's initial league. There were eight teams in the NL's introductory season, many of which still are around today in some form. They were the Boston Red Stockings, Chicago White Stockings, Cincinnati Reds, Hartford Dark Blues, Louisville Grays, New York Mutuals, Philadelphia Athletics, and St. Louis Brown Stockings. National League rules called for 70 regular season games to be played; however, only the Red Stockings actually accomplished that feat. Every other team played between 57 and 69 games.

Hulbert's White Stockings were far and away the most impressive team of the NL's first season, finishing the year with a 52-14 record, six games ahead of the Brown Stockings (45-19) and the Dark Blues (47-21). They went 33-3 against teams that finished the season with a record below .500. On the opposite end of the spectrum, the Reds lacked any success whatsoever, finishing the year at 9-56, 42.5 games back of their Chicago foes. Extrapolated to a modern 162 game season, that record translated to around 22-140.

While there was no official postseason in 1876 and the White Stockings officially won the regular season, Chicago and St. Louis unofficially squared off in the 1876 Championship of the West, which the George McManus-managed Browns won 4 games to 1. There would not be another postseason series held until 1882.

Notable births in 1876 include Rube Waddell, Mordecai Brown, Vic Willis, Elmer Flick, Frank Chance, and George Stone. Waddell, one of the game's first strikeout artists, led all MLB pitchers in strikeouts for five consecutive seasons in the early 20th century (tied with Randy Johnson for the most in baseball history) and won the Pitching Triple Crown in the American League in 1905. Despite the nickname "Three Finger," Mordecai Brown actually had four and a half fingers on his pitching hand, allowing him to get more movement on his pitches. Brown and first baseman Chance played a huge part in the Chicago Cubs' first two World Series titles. Willis, however, had more wins and more pitching WAR in his career than Waddell and Brown, finishing with 249 victories and 68.0 WAR in his 13 seasons. Flick, a speedy outfielder, was the first player to lead the American League in triples in three consecutive seasons. No player has done it four years in a row. Although he only played in five full seasons, George Stone had a terrific 1906 season, leading the AL in average, on-base percentage, and slugging percentage.

Hartford Dark Blues via Wikimedia Commons

Interesting numbers from the 1876 season:
- Ross Barnes of the White Stockings was far and away the best hitter in 1876. He slashed .429/.462/.590 (all league leaders), and also totaled an NL best 126 runs, 138 hits, 21 doubles, 14 triples, and 20 walks in only 66 games. His .429 batting average currently ranks as the third-best in Major League history, and his 235 OPS+ comes in at ninth all time. The only other second baseman in National League history to match Barnes' 1.052 OPS is Rogers Hornsby. Barnes also hit the NL's first home run, an inside-the-parker on May 2 in Cincinnati. It'd be one of two home runs that Barnes hit in his 234 game National League career.
- Since the White Stockings would eventually become the modern day Chicago Cubs, Barnes owns Cubs single-season

records for batting average and OPS+, while his .462 on-base percentage ranks second behind only King Kelly's .483 OBP in 1886. Barnes is one of two players to set a current franchise's single-season batting average record before the Modern Era, which began in 1893. Tip O'Neill, who set the Cardinals' single-season record in 1887 at .435, is the only other player to do so. No other player in Cubs franchise history has even batted .400 in a season.

- Ross Barnes boosted the league-wide OPS by seven points in 1876. If you remove his totals from the league stats, the NL average OPS drops from .598 to .591.

- As it was the first major league season, any league leading statistic in 1876 was also, at the time, a single-season record. Philadelphia's George Hall's five home runs was a Major League record that would stand until 1879. Hall also became the first major league player to hit multiple home runs in a single game.

- Similar to Hall's case, Chicago's Deacon White became the first ever hitter with 60 RBI in a season. White, primarily a catcher, is one of five backstops (Roy Campanella, Johnny Bench thrice, Gary Carter, Darren Daulton) to lead his league in runs batted in.

- Lip Pike hit more triples for the St. Louis Brown Stockings in 1876 than the entire St. Louis Cardinals team in 2018. Pike's ten triples were the third most in the National League in 1876, whereas the nine triples that the Cardinals hit in 2018 are an all-time low for the Cardinals franchise. It's important to note that these St. Louis Brown Stockings are not the beginning of the St. Louis Cardinals franchise— those St. Louis Brown Stockings would show up six years later as a part of the American Association.

- The oldest player to play a game in 1876 was Harry Wright, one of the founders of organized baseball in America. Born in 1835 (the same year as Mark Twain and Andrew Carnegie), the English-born outfielder went 0-for-3 in his sole game for the Red Stockings.
- Reds outfielder Emanuel "Redleg" Snyder sported a .151/.155/.176 slash line in 206 plate appearances. His 32 times reaching base safely are the second fewest among players with 200+ PA in a season (Gus Weyhing had 30 in 1891).
- Cal McVey of Chicago went on a massive hot streak in July of 1876. He had back-to-back six hit games, and in a four game span totaled a record 18 hits.
- The Chicago White Stockings as a whole batted an astounding .337 over the course of the season. Behind two 1894 teams, the White Stockings' mark is currently the third-best batting average by a team in a single season. The league batting average, not including Chicago, was .254. Their 146 OPS+ is the best by a team in a single season (the second-best in the NL that season was 104 by Philadelphia). To put a 146 OPS+ into perspective, imagine a team made up of players as dominant relative to the rest of the league as Jim Thome was in his career. The reason Chicago's OPS+ looks so good is because the league average OPS was only .598, while the White Stockings sat at .770. To us, a .770 OPS isn't anything remarkable, but it was in the run scoring era of 1876.
- White Stockings outfielder Paul Hines hit .331 in 1876, good for the eighth best in the National League out of 62 qualified hitters. However, his average was 6 points lower than his team's .337 BA.

13

- Batting average leaders for 1876:

```
.429 - Ross Barnes (Chicago White Stockings)
.366 - George Hall (Philadelphia Athletics)
.356 - Cap Anson (Chicago White Stockings)
.351 - John Peters (Chicago White Stockings)
.347 - Cal McVey (Chicago White Stockings)
.343 - Deacon White (Chicago White Stockings)
.340 - Levi Meyerle (Philadelphia Athletics)
.331 - Paul Hines (Chicago White Stockings)
```

- Chicago also allowed only 3.9 runs per game, a mark far below the league's average of 6.0. They outscored opponents by 367 runs in their 66 game season, or an average run differential of +5.56 runs per game, scaling to a pace of a run differential of +901 over the course of a 162 game season. If the Red Sox did not allow a single run in their 2018 World Series winning campaign, their run differential would've been a mere +876.
- Pitching statistics from way back in the day are a little wonky for a couple of reasons. First, the defense was so poor that there was an incredible disparity between the amount of runs scored (3,066) and the amount of earned runs scored (1,215). Next, and more important, is that earned runs and ERA were not official statistics in the National League until 1912, so all ERA figures before 1912 have been retroactively computed. The league's ERA was 2.31, but that doesn't really tell the whole story as teams scored an average of 6 runs per game.
- Leading all qualifiers was George Bradley with a 1.23 ERA. He pitched all but four of the St. Louis Brown Stockings' total innings that season, and his 16 shutouts are a single-season

mark that has never been topped. Bradley is the only player in Major League history to toss 500 innings with a sub-1.30 ERA in a season. Likewise, the Brown Stockings hold the record for the best team ERA in a season, at 1.22. The four non-Bradley innings came from outfielder Joe Blong, who did not allow a run. Bradley also tossed Major League Baseball's first no hitter, on July 15, 1876, against Hartford.

- Al Spalding of Chicago set a record with 47 wins on the season, which would not be broken until 1883. Spalding was also a co-founder of the A.G. Spalding sporting goods company and set a trend among players by wearing a baseball glove.

- Jim Devlin of Louisville tossed a league-leading 66 complete games and 622 innings. He struck out 122 batters, also an NL best. His 17.7 WAR currently ranks as the fourth-best ever by a player in a season, beating out every season that legends like Babe Ruth or Barry Bonds could muster. Baseball Reference computes Devlin's year to be worth 134 runs above average, 58 more than Hall of Famer Jack Morris totaled... in his entire 18 season career.

- Five Cincinnati pitchers were awarded a decision in 1876. Of them, Cherokee Fisher's 4-20 record, or .167 winning percentage, was the best. The other pitchers went 4-26, 1-8, 0-1, and 0-1. Fisher also allowed the National League's first home run (to Ross Barnes).

- Only 14 pitchers in the entire league had double-digit strike-out totals. The last *team* to not have 14 pitchers with double-digit strikeouts was the Reds in 2012.

- There were 260 games played in the inaugural season of the National League. Do you know how many of those games were started by a left-handed pitcher? The answer is zero.

There were 24 pitchers that started a game in 1876, all of whom were righties. In fact, 31 out of the 35 players who threw a pitch in 1876 were right-handed and, to this day, the throwing hands of the other four pitchers are unknown.
- On October 23, the *Chicago Tribune* published season statistics, including batting average, to the world for the first time.

As it was the first major league season, 1876's statistics seem otherworldly to a modern baseball fan. In no scenario would a manager let a player throw 66 complete games, nor is any one team dominant enough to bat .337 over the course of a season. Recording consecutive six hit games is unspeakable, as is a team with 1.22 ERA in an entire season. Now classified as extremes, 1876's numbers were nothing unique at the time; it was just how baseball was played. And it obviously worked well enough, as the National League still remains over 140 years later, unlike its predecessors.

1877

Only a year after baseball's first major league came its first minor league. The League Alliance consisted of 12 teams recruited by the National League. The NL consisted of only six teams this year: the Boston Red Stockings, Brooklyn Hartfords, Chicago White Stockings, Cincinnati Reds, Louisville Grays, and St. Louis Brown Stockings. The Red Stockings, at 42-18, finished in first place, posting a staggering 27-5 record at home. Chicago followed up its record setting 52-14 season with a 26-33 record, which placed them in fifth place in the league ahead of Cincinnati, who finished in last place for its second consecutive season. The Reds disbanded in mid-June as a result of a lack of funding, but were readmitted again only a few days later despite losing multiple players to other clubs. Will White, a pitcher for Boston, became the first professional player to wear glasses, while his teammate Tommy Bond demonstrated the legitimacy of the Candy Cummings-invented "curveball" by literally curving it around stakes that were driven into the ground before a game.

There was no postseason played in 1877; as a result, Boston was the National League Champion.

Players born in 1877 include Tommy Leach, one of four Pirates with 1,000 runs and 250 stolen bases in their tenure with the team, and Earl Moore, who went 20-8 with a 1.74 ERA at age 25 for Cleveland.

On October 1st, Ed Somerville died in London, Ontario, Canada. The 24-year-old Somerville was the first National League player to pass away. Somerville had a .406 OPS in 64 games for Louisville in '76.

The only player with 30 career WAR to debut in 1877 was the aforementioned Will White, who would lead the American Association in wins twice and ERA once in his ten-year career. White's 2.28 ERA is the third best in MLB history among pitchers with 400 career starts, behind only Christy Mathewson and Walter Johnson.

Cummings, Jim Devlin, and Harry Wright all played their final games in 1877. Cummings, who was 5'9" and 120 lbs and won 145 games including his NA days, was inducted into the Hall of Fame largely due to his claim to fame of inventing the curveball. Devlin led the National League in losses in his only two seasons in the league. Wright, son of an English cricket player, was most known for assembling baseball's first professional baseball team in 1869. He would be inducted into the Hall of Fame in 1953 as one of the game's pioneers.

via Wikimedia Commons

Interesting numbers from the 1877 season:
- Deacon White of the Boston Red Stockings (or the Red Caps, depending on where you look) led the league with a 193 OPS+. The current-day Atlanta Braves date all the way back to the Red Stockings, so when looking at Atlanta Braves franchise history, one must look all the way back into the 19th century. Thus, White's 193 OPS+ is the third best qualified season in Braves history, behind only Rogers Hornsby's 1928 campaign (202 OPS+) and Hank Aaron's 1971 campaign (194 OPS+). White is also the only player in Braves history to lead his league in batting average and RBI in the same season. Deacon White was the brother and teammate of then rookie Will White.
- Jim O'Rourke led the league with 68 runs scored in only 61

games played. In his career, O'Rourke averaged 140 runs scored per 162 games.

- Despite scoring 6.1 runs per game, the White Stockings failed to hit a home run in the 1877 season. They are the only team in MLB history to play 60 games and not hit a homer. The only other team to hit as few as one home run is the Brown Stockings, who also did it in the great year of 1877.
- Only 16 players hit a home run in 1877, tied with 1878 for the fewest in a season in MLB history.
- Louisville's Jim Devlin did something quite remarkable, something that had never been done at the time and will never be done again — he pitched every single inning for his team that season. He started and finished all 61 games played by the Grays that year, totaling 559 innings pitched and 13.2 pitching WAR. He also finished fifth on his team in hits for good measure. 1877 was Devlin's fifth and final season in professional baseball, as he and three of his teammates would be permanently banned from baseball after admitting to throwing games.
- Tommy Bond of Boston went 40-17 with a league leading 2.11 ERA. 1877 would be his first of three consecutive seasons with at least 40 wins, making him the only player in Major League history to put together three straight seasons of 40+ victories.
- Only two players accumulated even 4 WAR in 1877: Devlin (13.4, including a fraction of a win as a hitter) and Bond (11.4). The next-most valuable player after Bond was Deacon White at only 3.4.
- On July 13, George Bradley played a game at third base, ending his streak of 88 consecutive games on the mound.
- Pitchers Jim Devlin and Terry Larkin tied for the most losses

in the National League in 1877, yet both finished the season with a winning record. Devlin finished with a 35-25 record for the Louisville Grays, while Larkin's season with the Hartfords of Brooklyn ended with him posting a 29-25 record. Only two other pitchers have led the Majors in losses and finished with a winning record: Scott Perry in 1918 and Phil Niekro in 1979.

- 326 of the 360 starts in the 1877 season were complete games. The White Stockings' 15 games featuring a relief pitcher was the most, and represented almost half of the league's total.

Devlin's season is one of the most unique seasons from a statistical standpoint of all time. Pitching every inning for your team over an entire season more than exceeds the definition of a "workhorse". Nowadays, someone who pitches a few 30 start seasons in a row gets that title. The WAR concentration among the top two players is also incredible, as those two pitchers were heads and shoulders more valuable than the undisputed best hitter in the game that year. It makes sense, as pitchers who could throw for *literally* a full season provide way more value to their team than even the best of the best at the plate.

1878

Like in the season prior, the National League featured only six teams in 1878: Boston, Cincinnati, and Chicago as well as the Indianapolis Blues, Milwaukee Grays, and Providence Grays. Every team had a color in their name. Catapulted by their 21-3 record versus sub-.500 teams, Boston won their second consecutive pennant completing their schedule with a 41-19 record, while the Milwaukee Grays finished 26 games back in last place with a record of 15-45 in their only National League season. For the first time in NL history, every team played every game on their schedule, which consisted of 60 games.

Jimmy Sheckard, Bill Bradley, and Miller Huggins were all born in 1878. Sheckard stole an NL-leading 77 bases as a 20-year-old outfielder in 1899, while Bradley recorded an insane 60 sacrifice hits in 1908. While Huggins did lead the NL in walks four times, he's most known for managing the Yankees from 1918-1929, winning three World Series titles and six AL Pennants.

Jim McCormick, John Montgomery Ward, King Kelly, Charlie Bennett, and Ned Williamson all made their debuts in 1878. McCormick completed 466 of his 485 starts in his decade-long career, winning 265 contests. Ward, a stud pitcher who led the NL in ERA in his rookie season, would later transition to the field where he totaled over 2,000 hits for his career. "Monte" also founded the Players' League, another Major League which played its one season in 1890. Not only did King Kelly have a cool name, he also led the NL in runs in three consecutive seasons, totaling 399 from 1884-1886. Bennett caught for four pennant winning teams, while Williamson, most notably, would go on to hold the single-season home run record for over 30 years before it was broken by Babe Ruth.

Al Spalding retired in 1878. Including his time in the National Association, Spalding's .795 career winning percentage is the best of all time. He went 262-65, leading his league in wins in each year from 1871 to 1876. Spalding also batted .313 in his eight year career (only three of which came in the National League, however). Spalding created the first baseball rule book, and, according to his plaque in Cooperstown, was the "organizer of baseball's first round-the-world tour in 1888."

Interesting numbers from the 1878 season:
- Paul Hines, an outfielder for Providence, became the first hitter to win the Triple Crown. Hines led the National League with a .358 batting average, 4 home runs, and 50 runs batted in. Some argue that Hines also turned the first unassisted triple play in major league history in 1878, but many historians argue that one of the three outs recorded by Hines actually belonged to his teammate.
- With a 122 OPS+, Jim O'Rourke was the only player on the pennant-winning Red Stockings team to finish the season with an OPS+ over 100 (the league average). Boston went 41-19 on the season, winning 68.3% of their games. If you translate those two numbers into a 162 game season, you end

up with a 111-win team with just one above-average hitter.

- Joe Start's 100 hits for the Chicago White Stockings led the league, making him the owner of the lowest hit total by a league leader in Major League history.

- Rookie Russ McKelvy tied for the Major League lead in games played when he appeared in all 63 of the Indianapolis Blues' games in 1878. Four years later, McKelvy would play in the 64th and final game of his career as a member of the Pittsburgh Alleghenys.

- Boston's .253 OBP in 1878 is the lowest of any team that's ever finished a season with a winning record. For comparison, Hall of Fame *pitcher* Herb Pennock had a .253 OBP over his 22 year career. The Red Stockings' .253 OBP is the worst in Braves franchise history, but at the same time 1878 was the fourth highest winning percentage for a season in their history.

- Like 1877, only 16 players homered in the entire season; that's tied for the fewest in a season in MLB history. More than half of the teams in 2018 had 16 players hit a home run.

- 18-year-old rookie pitcher John Ward led the league with a 1.51 earned run average. Of the 11 pitchers to qualify for the ERA title in their age 18 season (or younger), Ward's 1.51 ERA is the best by more than eight tenths of a run.

- On May 9, Sam Weaver of Milwaukee tossed a no-hitter against Indianapolis for Milwaukee's first win in the National League. Although one scorer credited his opponent with a single rather than an error, most recognize Weaver's outing as a no-no. As this was Milwaukee's only season in the NL, and they only won 15 games, 6.7 percent of their franchise victories were no-hitters.

- The Boston Red Stockings won their championship using

only ten players for the entire season. One of whom, Harry Schafer, only appeared in 2 games.

1878 was a year of firsts. It featured the National League's first repeat champion, its first Triple Crown winner, arguably its first unassisted triple play (although probably not), and the first time that every scheduled game was actually played. It saw the debut of a future star in John Ward, and the retirement of one of the best nineteenth century pitchers in Albert Spalding.

1879

For the first time since the National League's inaugural season in 1876, the league was going back to eight teams. On March 24th, 1879, the National League made a move to adopt an eight-team, 84-game schedule for the upcoming season. The NL saw the arrival of the Buffalo Bison, Cleveland Blues, Syracuse Stars, and the Troy Trojans to their league and dealt with the departure of the Indianapolis Blues and Milwaukee Grays, a couple of one-and-done teams from the season before. The Providence Grays would post a 59-25 record with a run differential of more than +3 runs per game on their way to being crowned the champions.

Roger Bresnahan was born in 1879. He is the only player in MLB history to play 500 games at catcher and 200 games in center field in his career. Jim O'Rourke and Craig Biggio are the only other players to play even 200 at each in their career.

In 1879, the National League would see the debut of Dan Brouthers, a future Hall of Fame first baseman, and Jack Glasscock, arguably the best shortstop of the 19th century. Brouthers is one of six players in MLB history to win seven slugging titles in his career, while Glasscock led the National League in hits in back-to-back seasons in 1889 and 1890.

Tom Carey played the final game of his career in 1879. Carey was the starting second baseman for the Fort Wayne Kekiongas in the first ever National Association game, which was held on May 4th, 1871. The Kekiongas won that game 2-0 over the Cleveland Forest Citys.

Providence Grays via Wikimedia Commons

Interesting numbers from the 1879 season:
- On June 20th, Oscar Walker became the first Major Leaguer to strike out 5 times in a 9-inning game.
- Charley Jones hit 9 home runs on his way to becoming the new single-season home run record holder. Jones' teammate, John O'Rourke, hit 6 home runs as well, which would have been a new National League record if it wasn't for Charley's season. Both Jones and O'Rourke would set a new NL record for RBI with 62 apiece.

- Jim O'Rourke led the league with a .371 OBP and John O'Rourke, Jim's brother, led the league with a .521 SLG.
- With 14 triples on the year, Buttercup Dickerson was, and still is, the youngest player to lead the National League in triples. Buttercup, the left fielder for the Cincinnati Reds, turned 21 years of age on July 23rd of 1879.
- Paul Hines' 146 hits for the Providence Grays is a new single-season record. The record will only stand for 4 years, when an expanded schedule for the 1883 season allows for a new leader.
- Between his playing time for the Syracuse Stars and the Troy Trojans, catcher Bill Holbert totaled 50 hits in 1879. With all 50 of Holbert's hits being singles, he's the only player in Major League history to rack up that many hits in a season without recording an extra-base hit.
- Cincinnati Reds pitcher Will White would finish all 75 games in which he started, throwing 680 innings and 232 strikeouts on his way to a 1.99 ERA on the season. White's 75 complete games and 680 innings pitched will remain MLB records forever (or at least until robots take over). His .581 win-loss percentage (43-31-1) was the lowest by a National League pitcher with a sub-2.00 ERA and 200+ strikeouts in a season for the next 139 years; that honor now belongs to Jacob deGrom.
- Will White may have had an incredible season on the mound, but he was setting unwanted records at the plate at the same time. White went 40-for-294 at the plate in 1879, bad enough for a .136 batting average. That .136 average is still the worst single-season batting average by a qualified player in MLB history.
- Jim McCormick and George Bradley became the first 40-loss

pitchers in Major League history, despite having a 2.42 ERA
and a 2.85 ERA, respectively.

- After racking up 239 strikeouts on the season, 19-year-old
John Montgomery Ward became the youngest player to ever
hold the title of "single-season strikeout king." The only
teenagers to strike out more in a season? Amos Rusie (341 K's
in 1890), Bob Feller (240 K's in 1938), and Dwight Gooden
(276 K's in 1984).

About 9 weeks after the final game of the season, the National
League would hold their annual meeting in Buffalo. The following rule changes were discussed and then adopted:

- Walks would now require 8 balls, not 9.
- Catchers must catch the 3rd strike on the fly to record the
out.
- The final outs of the last half inning would not need to be
completed if the home team was already ahead (finally!).
- Baserunners were out if hit by a ball in play.

In addition to these rule changes, the National League adopted
a rule that would allow teams to suspend a player for the rest
of a season and the entire next season for drunkenness and/or
insubordination.

1880

Besides the Worcester Ruby Legs (also known as the Worcesters) and Cincinnati Stars replacing the Syracuse Stars and Cincinnati Reds, the league structure of the National League in 1880 looked like it did in 1879. The Chicago White Stockings won the National League pennant with little resistance from any other club, finishing with a record of 67-17, 15 games better than any other team. Their .798 winning percentage is the best in a season by any team in National League or American League history, and would translate to a 129-33 record over a 162 game season. Buffalo (24-58) and Cincinnati (21-59) would both finish over 40 games behind the White Stockings. 1880 saw a few rule changes as well, as mentioned in the previous chapter: eight balls were required for a walk instead of nine, baserunners were out if hit by a ball in play, and catchers were required to catch strike three for a strikeout to be recorded.

Notable players born in 1880 include Sam Crawford, Addie Joss, Christy Mathewson, and Joe Tinker. Crawford holds baseball's career triples record, while Joss holds that same title but for WHIP (walks plus hits per inning pitched). Mathewson is known for his elite postseason pitching and 373 career wins, but few know that he is one of three players (also Cy Young, Walter Johnson) to lead his league in strikeout-to-walk ratio in nine different seasons.

Tinker played fifteen seasons, all in Chicago with either the Cubs or the Federal League's Chi Feds or Whales.

Several stars debuted in 1880, including Tim Keefe, Roger Connor, Old Hoss Radbourn, Mickey Welch, Buck Ewing, Harry Stovey, and Fred Dunlap. Keefe, who you'll read about later in this section, posted the lowest ERA in a qualified season in MLB history. Connor held the career home run record until Babe Ruth would overtake him. Radbourn got as close to 60 wins in a season as anyone will ever get, finishing with a controversial 59 in 1884. Ewing, one of the most versatile players in the game's history, is one of just nine players to play 20+ games at each of catcher, first base, second base, third base, and shortstop in a career. Behind only Connor and Sam Thompson, Stovey's 122 homers were the third most in the 1800s. Meanwhile, Fred Dunlap's 185 hits in 1884 were the most in a season at the time. Overall, 1880 is one of five seasons in the history of baseball to see five future Hall of Fame players debut in the same season.

Interesting numbers from the 1880 season:
- Future Hall of Famer Cap Anson's 74 runs batted in became a new Major League record for a single season, topping Charley Jones and John O'Rourke's mark set a year prior.
- George Gore of Chicago slashed .360/.399/.463, all league bests, making him one of two players in Chicago Cubs franchise history to lead baseball in all three triple-slash stats in a season. (Ross Barnes in 1876 was the other.) Gore would play 12 more seasons and never lead the league in any of the three stats again.
- Abner Dalrymple, also of Chicago, became the second player in Major League history to score 90 runs in a season (also

joining Barnes' 1876). The White Stockings had three of the five top run scorers in the league in 1880.

- Boston's Charley Jones became the first player to hit two home runs in a single inning.
- John O'Rourke of Boston became the first player with four doubles in one game.
- Troy Trojans pitcher Tim Keefe set a "record" that has yet to be broken: lowest ERA in a qualified season. His 0.86 earned run average is one of only two sub-1.00 ERA seasons in history. Despite not pitching 500 innings like some of his counterparts at the time, his 105 innings pitched still qualifies him under modern rules (which require at least one inning pitched per game) for the all-time single-season ERA title. Keefe went 6-6 in 12 starts, all of which he completed. However, Major League Baseball does not actually recognize Keefe as holding the single-season ERA record because he did not start enough games, which was the requirement back in the day.
- Fred Goldsmith of, you guessed it, the White Stockings, finished 21-3, setting the single-season win percentage record at .875.
- Chicago's records didn't stop there. Larry Corcoran, a rookie pitcher, set MLB's strikeout record at 268, topping the previous record of 239 set by John Ward in the previous season. Corcoran is now one of seven rookies to record 250 strikeouts in a season. Corcoran and the aforementioned Goldsmith are considered the first pitching rotation in Major League history.
- Worcester's Lee Richmond tossed the first perfect game in MLB history on June 12 in a 1-0 win over Cleveland.
- Six days later, John Ward tossed the second perfect game in MLB history over Buffalo. The National League would not

see another perfect game for more than 80 years.

- Lee Richmond pitched in 74 of the Worcester Ruby Legs' 85 games in the 1880 season. His 74 games pitched would remain a MLB rookie record for the next 89 years.
- The White Stockings won 21 consecutive games, a record that would stand until September of 1916.

The White Stockings simply dominated baseball in 1880. Not only did they have a historic win-loss record and 21-game winning streak, but also had several players set individual records. Baseball also saw the best single-season ERA in its history, the first two perfect games, and the births and debuts of several baseball legends.

1881

The 1881 season once again consisted of an eight-team, 84-game schedule with seven of those teams returning from the year before. In December of 1880, Detroit was elected to take over the vacancy in the league that was abandoned by the now defunct Cincinnati Reds/Stars. The Wolverines would become Detroit's representative in the National League. The Wolverines would have a fairly successful inaugural season, finishing with a near .500 record, but the season once again belonged to the Chicago White Stockings. The White Stockings (56-28) had now joined the Boston Red Stockings as the only teams to win back-to-back championships.

1881 saw the birth of four Hall of Famers: Johnny Evers, Ed Walsh, Branch Rickey, and Will Harridge. Evers, a second baseman, was certainly not known for his power, hitting only a dozen home runs in his 1,784 game career. Ed Walsh, meanwhile, owns the best career ERA in MLB history. Rickey only played in four seasons as a big leaguer; he is most known for his work as an executive, including when he signed Negro League star Jackie Robinson in 1945. Harridge served as president of the American League for nearly 30 years.

Tony Mullane debuted in 1881; his 343 wild pitches are the most of all time. Mullane also had five 30-win seasons. We mentioned that Old Hoss Radbourn made his debut in 1880, but that was as a position player. Radbourn didn't make his pitching debut until 1881, after being signed by the Providence Grays as a free agent on February 7. Radbourn's 309 career wins lands him in the top twenty of the all-time leaderboard.

Ross Barnes played in his final game on September 21, 1881. His .429 batting average from the 1876 season would remain the highest single-season batting average in the National League for 18 years until Hugh Duffy put up a .440 batting average in 1894, lowering Barnes' .429 BA into second place, where it remains today. Barnes starred in the National Association, where he had a 185 OPS+ in five seasons.

Interesting numbers from the 1881 season:
- Roger Connor hit the first grand slam in National League history. The home run came with the Troy Trojans trailing 7-4 in the bottom of the 9th inning and with 2 outs already recorded. Of course, baseball's first grand slam was of the "ultimate" variety.
- On June 25th, Chicago's George Gore stole second base five times and third base twice in a game versus Providence. The seven stolen bases in a game remain a record today, only matched one other time in MLB history, by Billy Hamilton on August 31, 1894.
- After setting the single-season record for RBI in 1880, Chicago's Cap Anson improved on his record by driving in 82 runs, 8 more than the year before. Anson's 82 RBI in 1881 would propel him past Cal McVey on the career RBI leaderboard, a place where his name would reside for the

next 52 years until Babe Ruth eventually passed him.

- Cap Anson put up a 5.9 WAR season in 1881, making this his second consecutive season leading the National League in position player WAR, becoming the first to lead the NL in position player WAR twice. Following that season, Anson would also become the all-time leader in position player WAR. The 30.3 career WAR that Cap had accumulated by the end of the 1881 season would only account for a little over 32% of his final career total of 94.3 WAR.
- Pitcher Pud Galvin broke the strikeout record … as a hitter. His 70 strikeouts were thirteen more than anyone else had ever had in a season up until that point. His record would stand until 1883.
- At the time, Dan Brouthers' eight home runs in 1881 were the most in a season by a left-handed hitter. Brouthers would become one of just three lefties with 100 career homers before the start of the Live Ball Era in 1920, Mike Tiernan and Hall of Famer Sam Thompson were the other two.
- Boston rookie Jim Whitney finished the season with a 31-33 record, becoming the first pitcher to lead the league in wins AND losses. It'd be 98 years until that feat was duplicated, when Phil Niekro finished the 1979 season with a 21-20 record for the Atlanta Braves.
- Lee Richmond finished 50 of his 52 starts for the Ruby Legs. To go along with his 57 complete games the season before, Richmond is (and always will be) the only left-handed pitcher to toss 50 complete games in multiple seasons.

With the conclusion of the 1881 season, the National League had already become the longest-lasting and most successful professional baseball league in history. Those first 6 seasons had given baseball so many firsts. Many records were made and broken, some of which still exist today.

In preparation for the next season, the NL announced that all eight teams would be returning for the 1882 season, a first for the young league. Another first was on its way in 1882 as well, in the form of a rival league.

1882

1882 saw baseball's first real expansion. The American Association was founded, with six clubs: the Baltimore Orioles (who would die off in 1899), Cincinnati Red Stockings (who would later become the modern Reds), Louisville Eclipse (died off in 1899), Philadelphia Athletics (died off in 1890), Pittsburgh Alleghenys (who would later become the modern Pirates), and the St. Louis Brown Stockings (who would later become the modern Cardinals). Chicago would once again finish with the best record in the National League, at 55-29, while Worcester was by far the worst team in the league, finishing at 18-66, 18.5 games behind the next worst team. In the AA's inaugural season, Cincinnati easily won the AA regular season at 55-29. Baltimore finished last at 19-54. In the first resemblance of a playoff series since 1876, the White Stockings tied the Red Stockings in an exhibition series at one game apiece. Louisville's Tony Mullane became the first "switch pitcher," pitching with his left hand to left-handed batters and with his right hand to right-handed batters.

Babe Adams, Pete Hill, Ed Reulbach, Red Ames, Jack Coombs, and Frank Schulte were all born in 1882. In over 800 innings from 1919-1922, Adams walked only 74 batters. He was also a World Series winner with Pittsburgh sixteen years apart, winning as a 27-year-old in 1909 and as a 43-year-old in 1925. Reulbach, a pitcher for the Cubs during their peak in the early 1900s, went 60-15 with a 1.82 ERA from 1906-1908. Ames pitched in parts of seventeen seasons, totaling 183 victories and 1,702 strikeouts. Coombs led the Majors in wins in consecutive seasons (1910-1911) with the Athletics, going 59-21 with a 2.39 ERA in the span. "Wildfire" Schulte is most known for his 1911 season in which he had 30 doubles, 21 triples, and 21 home runs as the Cubs right fielder.

William Hulbert, founder of the National League and president of the Chicago White Stockings, passed away at the age of 49. It would take well over a century before the Veterans Committee of 1995 would induct Hulbert into the Hall of Fame.

Notable players to debut in 1882 include John Clarkson, Charlie Buffinton, Bid McPhee, Pete Browning, Guy Hecker, and Charlie Comiskey. It'd be less than half of a decade before Clarkson would lead baseball with 53 wins and 308 strikeouts. Buffinton, one of baseball's most underrated pitchers, totaled 60.7 WAR in his eleven seasons. McPhee, a career Red, has the fourth most hits in franchise history with 2,258. Browning had one of the best rookie seasons in MLB history (see below), while Hecker is unique in that he won a victory title, an ERA title, and a *batting* title all in a three-year span.

Baseball pioneer George Wright, brother of Harry, played his final game in 1882. He led the National League in plate appearances in each of its first two seasons.

Via Wikimedia Commons

Interesting numbers from the 1882 season:
- Louisville rookie infielder Pete Browning finished the season with an unbelievable 223 OPS+. At 21 years old, he is the youngest player with a 220 OPS+ in a season (the next

youngest player is Ted Williams, at age 22 in 1941). Browning also remains the only rookie in MLB history to post a 200 OPS+ in a season.

- Cap Anson led baseball in runs batted in for the third season in a row, with 83 RBI in 82 games. The only other players to lead baseball in RBI in three consecutive seasons? Babe Ruth and Cecil Fielder.

- Buffalo's Charles Foley became the first player to hit for the cycle in a game, as well as becoming the first player to hit multiple grand slams in one season.

- In a July game, the White Stockings beat the Cleveland Blues 35-4, with seven different Chicago players totaling four hits and four runs apiece.

- Jim O'Rourke would temporarily become baseball's home run king, finishing the year with 24 career home runs, the most by a player in MLB history.

- Alleghenys pitcher Denny Driscoll posted a 218 ERA+ in 1882, by far the best in Pirates franchise history. The next best qualified ERA+ in their franchise's history is 169 by John Candelaria in 1977.

- Louisville rookie Guy Hecker set an MLB record with his 0.769 WHIP. His mark would stand until Pedro Martinez would break it in 2000, with his 0.737 mark. Hecker's season currently slots in at second best all time, and first among rookies.

- In their inaugural season, the Louisville Eclipse became the first franchise with two no-hitters to their credit when Tony Mullane and the aforementioned Hecker threw no-nos just eight days apart. Rookie Dan Sullivan was the catcher for both of the no-hitters, which were thrown on September 11th and 19th, making him the first catcher to be behind the plate for two no-nos. Sullivan would hold that honor all to himself for a grand total of one day.

- On September 20th, Larry Corcoran tossed his second no-hitter of his career, the first pitcher with multiple such games in Major League history. Corcoran's catcher Silver Flint joined Sullivan as the first two catchers to be behind the dish for two no-hitters. This was the White Stockings' second no-hitter for their franchise, making the team *and* catcher Silver Flint a day late from being the first to multiple no-no's.

- Flint also became the first position player to strike out 50 times in a single season. Previously, only pitchers Will White and Pud Galvin had crossed the 50 mark in a season.

- Jim McCormick of Cleveland became the first pitcher to walk 100 batters in a season. He walked 103, and struck out 200 in 595.2 innings.

- A year after both winning and losing 30 games, Jim Whitney batted .323/.382/.510 in 275 plate appearances, leading the Red Stockings with five home runs and tying for their lead with 24 walks drawn. Whitney also led the team in wins, ERA, and strikeouts as a pitcher. Whitney would finish his career with eighteen home runs and a 112 OPS+ in 2,306 plate appearances. 1882 was the first time a pitcher hit five home runs; Whitney would repeat with another five in 1883. He finished tied for fifth in the Majors in homers in '82.

- Harry Arundel tossed 119 innings for the Pittsburgh Alleghenys, striking out 48 of the 189 (25.4%) batters he would face. Arundel became the first pitcher to ever throw 100 innings in a season and have a strikeout rate higher than 25%. It would be another 73 years before Herb Score would become the second pitcher to ever do this.

- Denny Driscoll, Arundel's teammate, set a still-standing

Pirates franchise record with his 1.21 ERA. Driscoll started and completed 23 games, allowing only 27 earned runs in his 201.0 innings. He did, however, allow 46 unearned runs.

- Also setting a team ERA record was Harry McCormick, who allowed 37 earned runs (and 50 unearned runs) in 219.2 innings for the Cincinnati Red Stockings. His 1.52 ERA is the best in a qualified season in Reds history. His teammate, Will White, just missed out on this record, finishing with a 1.54 ERA. White's season was superior, however, as he pitched 480 innings, completing 52 games and going 40-12. McCormick, who finished the season 14-11, would've needed to go an additional 26-1 to match White's W-L record.
- The St. Louis Brown Stockings of the American Association became the first team to send 10 different pitchers to the mound in one season. Fast forward 133 years to 2015, and we'd see the Colorado Rockies use 13 pitchers in one game!

With the creation of the American Association, the amount of teams in the Majors nearly doubled. The baseball world saw the births of a few teams that still exist today, an attempt at a postseason series, the first switch pitcher, and the first cycle.

1883

In 1883, the New York Gothams and Philadelphia Quakers replaced the Troy Trojans and Worcester Ruby Legs/Worcesters, and the Boston Red Stockings became known as the Beaneaters. In the AA, the New York Metropolitans and Columbus Buckeyes joined the league, evening the Association and National League at eight teams apiece. Boston's 63-35 record topped the National League, while the Philadelphia Athletics' 66-32 record narrowly beat the Browns' 65-33 record for tops in the AA. The Philadelphia Quakers (17-81) and Baltimore Orioles (28-68) finished at the bottom of the NL and AA, respectively. The Athletics declined to play the Beaneaters in an interleague playoff series.

Jack Quinn and Hal Chase were born in 1883. Quinn, one of two Slovakian-born players in MLB history, would appear in at least ten games as a 25-year-old rookie in 1909 and as a 49-year-old veteran in 1933 (and several times in between). Chase, a Californian, won the NL batting title in 1916 for Cincinnati.

Jim Devlin, the only player to throw every inning for his team in a season, died of tuberculosis. He faced a staggering 4,896 batters in a two-year span.

Dave Orr and Tip O'Neill made their debuts in 1883. Orr is one of three players in MLB history with 30 triples in a season, while O'Neill put together one of the most dominant campaigns in early MLB history with his Triple Crown-winning 1887 season as a left fielder. However, O'Neill began his MLB career as a pitcher, going 5-12 with a 4.07 ERA as a rookie for the Giants.

Interesting numbers from the 1883 season:

- For the second consecutive season, Dan Brouthers led the National League in each triple-slash stat, hitting .374/.397/.572. He set the then single-season records in hits, total bases, and RBI, with 159 H, 243 TB, and 97 RBI in only 98 games. Brouthers also led all position players with his 5.8 wins above replacement.
- Jim O'Rourke's claim to fame of being baseball's Home Run King came to a quick end, as Charley Jones retook his spot as the King with a total of 33 career home runs to his name. O'Rourke would actually drop to third on the all-time home run list by the end of the 1883 season.
- Moving into second place on the all-time home run list with 27 round trippers was Harry Stovey, whose 14 home runs in 1883 were a new single-season record. It was the second time of four that Stovey would lead all of baseball in home runs for a season.
- Charlie Bennett posted a 150 OPS+ for the third consecutive season. The only other catcher in MLB history to string together three such seasons in a row? That'd be Mike Piazza, who did it in four consecutive seasons from 1995 to 1998.
- Chicago set a couple of crazy records in 1883. In their 31-7 July victory over Buffalo, they set a nine inning record with 14 doubles. A couple of months later, they set an MLB record by scoring 18 runs in the seventh inning of a game.

- Tim Keefe had what could be argued as the best single-season performance in MLB history. As a pitcher, he totaled 19.8 wins above replacement, going 41-27 with a record-setting 359 strikeouts. He also led the American Association in innings pitched (619.0), WHIP (0.963), and hits allowed per 9 innings (7.1). His 20.2 WAR that season (including his hitting) is the best mark in MLB history and barring a significant change in the game, will remain that way forever. Since 1930, the best WAR in a season is 13.3 by Dwight Gooden in 1985. 20.2 WAR represents 11 percent of Babe Ruth's career total.
- Keefe allowed six home runs over the course of the 1883 season. Fittingly, half of them were hit by the aforementioned Stovey.
- Jim Whitney of the Beaneaters led the National League with 345 punchouts. His strikeout-to-walk ratio of 9.86 remains the best among the 67 seasons in which a major league pitcher has recorded 300+ strikeouts. Curt Schilling's 2002 season (9.58 K:BB) and Pedro Martinez's 1999 season (8.46 K:BB) are ranked second and third on the list.
- Al Spalding's single-season record of 47 wins, set in the first year of the National League, was finally topped. Old Hoss Radbourn picked up 48 winning decisions for the Providence Grays on his way to setting the new top mark.
- A year after just missing out on the Reds' single-season ERA record, Red Stockings starter Will White won a franchise record 43 games. Along with his 40 from 1882, he owns the only two seasons with 35 wins in Reds franchise history.
- On the opposite side of the spectrum, baseball saw one of its least successful seasons of all time. John Coleman, a Quakers rookie pitcher/outfielder, set single-season records that still stand today: 48 losses, 772 hits allowed, and 291 earned

runs allowed. He won just twelve games, and also had an underwhelming .579 OPS in 369 plate appearances.

- John Ward, now of the New York Gothams, became the first pitcher to hit multiple home runs in a single game. He would hit a career high seven home runs in 1883. Ward would later become a full time outfielder following an injury to his right arm.
- Curry Foley picked up a win in his only pitching appearance of the season, striking out none in his one inning of relief. A couple seasons earlier, Foley picked up three wins despite only having two strikeouts on the year. He's one of only two players to ever have more wins than strikeouts in multiple seasons. That other player? Babe Ruth.

A year of extremes, 1883 saw records set that will likely never be broken. Baseball saw the single-season WAR record, as well as the loss, hits allowed, and earned runs allowed records. Radbourn's win record, on the other hand, wouldn't stand for long, nor would Stovey's home run record. However, at the time, they were the best ever seen in Major League Baseball.

1884

Didn't think 1882's addition of the American Association was a lot? Well, 1884 has got you covered. The Union Association, which lasted for exactly one season as a Major League, made an appearance in 1884. Millionaire Henry Lucas founded it, and also ran the St. Louis Maroons franchise. This caused an insanely lopsided distribution of talent, forcing teams to fold midseason. The Maroons, however, finished 94-19 and won the league. Since the league amounted to almost nothing, we won't give you a list of all the teams that attempted to beat the Maroons, but it might be worth noting that a team called the Milwaukee Brewers went 8-5. The American Association also added some teams: the Toledo Blue Stockings, Brooklyn Atlantics, Richmond Virginians, Indianapolis Hoosiers, and Washington Nationals. All the newly founded AA teams finished below .500, while the New York Metropolitans won the pennant at 75-32. In the National League, the Providence Grays bested the league with their 84-28 record. In the first ever World's Championship Series, the Grays knocked off New York three games to none. Also, 1884 marked the first season in NL history in which pitchers were permitted to throw overhand if they wished.

Births in 1884 include Chief Bender, Pop Lloyd, Eddie Cicotte, and Sherry Magee. Bender has the second most innings pitched in Athletics franchise history, behind only Eddie Plank. Lloyd is seen as one of the greatest shortstops in Negro League history. Cicotte totaled 58.4 WAR in his career, but would be one of the players suspended for throwing the 1919 World Series. Magee, who played on the other end of that World Series for the Reds, also led the NL in BA, OBP, and SLG in 1910.

Baseball would see the debut of Bob Caruthers, who was one of two pitchers with multiple 40-win seasons through age 25.

Tommy Bond retired, and also topped Bob Caruthers in the aforementioned stat. Bond won 40 games at age 21, 40 at age 22, and 43 at age 23.

Providence Grays via Wikimedia Commons

Interesting numbers from the 1884 season:
- The Chicago White Stockings set a record with 142 home runs on the season, destroying the old record of 34 set by the Cincinnati Red Stockings (AA) and Boston Beaneaters (NL) just a year earlier. Chicago's 142 dingers in 1884 would remain the most by a team for 43 years, even surviving 7 years of the Live Ball Era before the powerful 1927 New York Yankees would claim that top spot. Home runs were generally pretty scarce during the 19th century, but Chicago issued a ground rule change that would allow balls hit over the fence as home runs instead of doubles. The fences were less than 200 feet from home plate. 1884 would be Chicago's final season at Lakefront Park.
- Single-season HR leaderboard through the 1884 season:

```
27 - Ned Williamson (1884 White Stockings)
25 - Fred Pfeffer (1884 White Stockings)
22 - Abner Dalrymple (1884 White Stockings)
21 - Cap Anson (1884 White Stockings)
14 - Dan Brouthers (1884 Bisons)
14 - Harry Stovey (1883 Athletics)
13 - King Kelly (1884 White Stockings)
13 - Fred Dunlap (1884 Maroons)
```

- The five White Stockings players on that list combined for eight home runs on the road. The other 79 came at their friendly home ballpark.
- Ned Williamson's record of 27 home runs in a season would stand until 1919, when some guy named Babe Ruth came along. Through 1883, Williamson had hit eight home runs in

2086 plate appearances. In '84, he hit 27 homers in 459 trips to the plate. He would hit only 29 home runs in 2537 PA over the rest of his career after 1884. Talk about an outlier.

- White Stockings splits in 1884:

```
Home: 39-17 W-L, 498 R scored, 312 R allowed,
      21 games of 10+ runs, 1 with 0 or 1
Road: 23-33 W-L, 336 R scored, 334 R allowed,
      9 games with 10+ runs, 7 with 0 or 1
```

- Harry Stovey finished the 1884 season with ten home runs. Stovey, at the time, was the only Major Leaguer to hit double-digit HR totals in multiple seasons.
- Buck Ewing of the Gothams finished the season with 20 triples. At the time of writing this book, there have been 113 occasions in which a player has racked up 20+ three-baggers in a season, Ewing's 1884 season is the only one on the record books for a player whose primary position was catcher.
- Aided by weaker competition in the Union Association, Maroons second baseman Fred Dunlap would wind up leading all players with a .412 batting average. Dunlap's 185 hits became a new record for a season, topping the old record set by Dan Brouthers last year. Dunlap's 7.9 WAR and 160 runs scored also both set new single-season high marks for position players, replacing Ross Barnes' 6.0 WAR season in which he scored 126 runs back in 1876.
- Over the course of the season, Dunlap averaged scoring 1.58 runs per game played. The only other players in MLB history to average 1.50 R/G in a season with at least 50 games played

are Ross Barnes in 1876 (126 runs in 66 games) and Billy Hamilton in 1894 (198 runs in 132 games).

- Dunlap's 160 runs scored remains a record by a middle infielder, narrowly beating out shortstop Hughie Jennings' mark of 159 runs scored in 1895.
- Sam Wise becomes the first hitter to strike out 100 times in a season. His 104 strikeouts with the 1884 Boston Beaneaters would remain a record for 20 years.
- Teammates with a 200 OPS+ in the same season:

```
Fred Dunlap (256) & Orator Shafer (201)
        of the 1884 St. Louis Maroons
Lou Gehrig (220) & Babe Ruth (225)
        of the 1927 New York Yankees
Lou Gehrig (203) & Babe Ruth (211)
        of the 1930 New York Yankees
```

- From 1876 to 1883, professional baseball saw 699 home runs hit by 165 different players. In 1884, there were 689 home runs hit by 208 different players.
- The Kansas City Cowboys, who finished with a record of 16-63 in the UA, batted .199 as a team. They're the only Major League team with a sub-.200 batting average in a season of at least 50 games. Of the *51 players* that batted at least once for Kansas City, only five batted .300 or better: Emmett Seery (.500 in 2 AB), Ed Callahan (.364 in 11 AB), Ted Sullivan (.333 in 9 AB), Thomas Gorman (.321 in 106 AB), and Dick Blaisdell (.313 in 16 AB). Also, those 51 players are tied with the Washington Nationals of the same season for the most players used in a season by a team in the 19th Century.

- Mickey Welch of the New York Gothams finished the 1884 season with 345 strikeouts, good enough for the eighth most strikeouts in a season by a pitcher in National League history. Those 345 strikeouts were also good enough for fourth most in the National League... in 1884. However, Welch's 345 strikeouts remain the Giants franchise record today (the Gothams would become the New York Giants, who would later relocate to San Francisco).
- Most strikeouts in a season - National League history (keep in mind the NL's new rule allowing overhand pitching):

```
441 - Old Hoss Radbourn (1884 Providence Grays)
417 - Charlie Buffinton (1884 Boston Beaneaters)
382 - Sandy Koufax (1965 Los Angeles Dodgers)
372 - Randy Johnson (2001 Arizona Diamondbacks)
369 - Pud Galvin (1884 Buffalo Bisons)
```

- Buffinton's 417 strikeouts are a Braves franchise record for a single season.
- Guy Hecker (52-20 record) becomes the only pitcher in American Association history (1882-1891) to win the Pitching Triple Crown. He'd strike out 385 batters and post a 1.80 ERA in 75 games for the Louisville Eclipse.
- Hecker wasn't the only Triple Crown winner in '84. Old Hoss Radbourn's 59 wins, 1.38 ERA, and 441 strikeouts all led the National League. Radbourn and Tommy Bond (1877) were the first two pitching Triple Crown winners in National League history.
- Radbourn's 59 wins destroyed the old record of 48, a record that Old Hoss himself had just set in the previous season.

Some historians believe that his actual win total for the 1884 season should have been 60 wins, the total he was originally given credit for. Why? On July 28th, the Providence Grays and starting pitcher Cyclone Miller were losing a game by a score of 4-3 through five innings of play. Then, the Grays scored four runs in the top of the sixth to take a 7-4 lead. Radbourn relieved Miller to begin the bottom of the sixth inning and pitched a solid four innings of relief to hold on to the victory. By definition, Radbourn's outing that day earned him an official save, but some believe the official scorer would have given Old Hoss the victory since the Grays were losing the game the last time the starting pitcher was standing on the mound. As cool as 60 wins sounds, we're sticking with 59 as our record, the single-season record that stands today.

- White Stockings hurler Larry Corcoran allowed 35 home runs on the season. Prior to the 1884 season, no pitcher had allowed more than 32 home runs in their entire National League *career*. Of those 35 home runs, 29 came at his homer-friendly home ballpark.

- Larry McKeon struck out 308 hitters for the Indianapolis Hoosiers and Ed Morris struck out 302 for the Columbus Buckeyes. McKeon and Morris are two of only three pitchers to strike out 300+ in their rookie season. The only other rookie to reach the 300 strikeout mark is Matt Kilroy, who set the all-time single-season record with 513 strikeouts as a rookie for the 1886 Baltimore Orioles.

- Hugh "One Arm" Daily, who was nicknamed following a gun accident earlier in his life, struck out 483 batters (in the Union Association). His 8.7 strikeouts per 9 innings pitched would remain a single-season record until 1955, and his total of 483 strikeouts is still the most thrown in a single season by a right-handed pitcher.

- With his 20.5 pitching WAR season for the Buffalo Bisons, Pud Galvin put up arguably the most valuable season by a pitcher in the history of baseball. He would finish the year with a 46-22 record, 369 strikeouts, 12 shutouts, and a 1.99 ERA. Galvin is recognized today as the first player to be known for using performance enhancing substances. Galvin was actually applauded for his use of the Brown-Séquard Elixir, which contained monkey testosterone, before a game. Despite his known attempt to gain a competitive edge, Galvin would be inducted into the Baseball Hall of Fame in 1965.

- Only 5 teams have played 100+ games in a season and had their pitching staff post a sub-1.000 WHIP. The 1884 Providence Grays, St. Louis Maroons, Louisville Eclipse, and New York Metropolitans make up 80% of that list. The only other team to do this was the 1888 St. Louis Browns.

- On May 22nd, Wally Andrews made his debut and at 6'3" (190 cm), joining Roger Connor and John Reilly as the tallest players to ever play baseball. Three months later, on August 22nd, Jay Faatz, a 6'4" (193 cm) first baseman, made his first appearance and claimed sole possession of the title of tallest ballplayer. Faatz would lose that record 39 days later to Anton Falch of the Milwaukee Brewers. At 6'6" (198 cm), Falch would maintain at least a share of the record for nearly 29 years.

Three professional baseball leagues sure did provide for one of the craziest years in history. The National League expanded their schedule to 112 games, leading to many new counting stat records. In the American Association, Fleet Walker and then eventually his brother, Welday Walker, would become the first black players to ever play in the Major Leagues; both would play for the Toledo Blue Stockings. We can thank the Union Association for providing baseball history with team names such as the Quicksteps, Monumentals, Keystone, Maroons, and Outlaw Reds. In 1884, there were three more teams that played Major League baseball than there are in the Majors today, assuming an expansion hasn't happened by the time you're reading this book!

1885

After the failure of the Union Association, founder and Maroons owner Henry Lucas purchased what was left of the Cleveland Blues franchise (they released all of their players and essentially disbanded), and moved his Maroons to the National League, replacing Cleveland. 1885 saw the first year of overhand pitching in the American Association, a year after NL pitchers were given the opportunity. In 1884, AA pitchers were allowed to use a modified sidearm. The American Association was down to eight teams again: St. Louis, Cincinnati, Pittsburgh, Philadelphia, Brooklyn, Louisville, New York, and Baltimore. The NL saw the same eight teams from the year prior, except for the aforementioned St. Louis Maroons. The New York Gothams also became known as the New York Giants, the same name they possess today in the Bay Area. In the second ever World's Championship Series, the NL champion White Stockings (87-25) tied the AA champion Browns (79-33) 3-3-1. The first game was called for darkness. The White Stockings had to play their first 24 games on the road waiting for their new ballpark to be constructed; they went 18-6 in that span. Also of note, John Ward and teammates formed the first ever union in professional sports history.

Art Fletcher, Ed Konetchy, "Smokey" Joe Williams, and Jose

Mendez were born in 1885. Fletcher, who wasn't anything spectacular at the plate, did manage to lead the NL in hit by pitches five times in a six-year stretch. Konetchy totaled over 2,000 hits and 3,000 total bases in his 15 season career. Williams and Mendez would be inducted into the Baseball Hall of Fame for their Negro League careers.

Hall of Famer Sam Thompson, owner of baseball's first 20 home run, 20 stolen base season, made his debut in 1885. Thompson also racked up 166 RBI in 1897.

Interesting numbers from the 1885 season:
- Harry Stovey's league leading 13 home runs in 1885 made him the first player to reach 50 career home runs, also giving him the temporary title of Home Run King.
- The first player to ___ home runs:

```
 50: Harry Stovey
150: Babe Ruth
250: Babe Ruth
350: Babe Ruth
450: Babe Ruth
550: Babe Ruth
650: Babe Ruth
750: Hank Aaron
```

- New York first baseman Roger Connor's 8.2 WAR became an MLB record for position players. His .371 batting average and .435 on-base percentage paced all players in 1885 as well. He walked 51 times to only eight strikeouts.

58

- 42-year-old Providence first baseman Joe Start totaled 100 hits for the fifth consecutive season. He is one of seven players in MLB history with five seasons of 100+ hits from age 38 on. The others are Cap Anson (eight), Pete Rose (seven), Jim O'Rourke, Honus Wagner, Carl Yastrzemski, and Carlton Fisk. Start was the oldest player to play in 1885 by nearly five years.

- Pete Browning led the American Association in batting for the second time in his career, posting a .362 BA for the 1885 Louisville Colonels. Browning now owned a career .352 BA through his age 24 season. Among the 510 players to have at least 1,500 plate appearances prior to their age 25 season, only Ted Williams (.356), Ty Cobb (.359), and Wee Willie Keeler (.373) had a higher batting average than Browning.

- To this day, second baseman Joe Gerhardt's .155 average in 399 at bats in '85 remains the worst batting average by a player with at least 350 at bats in a season. Likewise, Charlie Bastian's .167 average in 1885 remains the worst by a shortstop (with the same at bat qualifier) in a season.

- On June 25, George Strief of the Athletics became the first of two players in MLB history with four triples in a single game, Bill Joyce in 1897 being the other. Strief would finish his modest five-year career with four of his fourteen triples coming in just one of his 362 career games.

- Charlie Bennett posted his fourth qualified season in his career with a 150 OPS+. The only other catcher with as many such seasons in a career is Mike Piazza, who had six in his career.

- On July 27th, John Clarkson threw the only no-hitter of his career, as his White Stockings would blank the Providence Grays by a score of 4-0. Clarkson's battery-mate that day was

Silver Flint, who became the first catcher in Major League history to get behind the plate for three no-hitters. Flint had previously been the backstop for Larry Corcoran's first two career no-hitters in 1880 and 1884. Only Jason Varitek and Carlos Ruiz have caught more no-hitters than Silver Flint; they have four each.

- Quakers player Charlie Ferguson went 26-20 with a 2.22 ERA, and also hit .306/.368/.379. In addition to his 48 pitching appearances, the Philadelphia two-way player appeared in 15 games in the outfield.

- The Giants pitching staff owned a 1.72 ERA over the course of the season compared to a 3.03 league-wide ERA. Their team ERA+ of 159 is the fifth best mark by a team in Major League history. Their starters Tim Keefe (1.58) and Mickey Welch (1.66) finished first and second in the MLB ERA race. They combined to pitch 892 of the team's 994 innings.

- Brooklyn Grays pitcher and self nicknamed John "Phenome-nal" Smith once bragged that he was so talented that he could win a game all by himself (although, at the time, Smith had never won a game in the Majors). On June 17, his teammates intentionally committed 14 errors, causing him to lose 18-5 before being promptly released for "team harmony" reasons.

From a stat perspective, 1885 could not come close to matching 1884 in terms of excitement. Baseball saw a tied World's Championship and all-time low batting averages. However, with overhand pitching permitted in both leagues, the game was due for some crazy pitching records.

1886

In 1886, a new statistic was born: the stolen base. A new rule change was brought about in the American Association, reducing the numbers of balls required for a walk to six. The National League stayed at seven for the time being. In the NL, the Buffalo Bisons and Providence Grays were replaced by the Kansas City Cowboys and the Washington Nationals, while the American Association kept its eight teams from a year prior. The Chicago White Stockings once again took home the NL pennant with a 90-34 record, as did the 93-46 Browns in the AA. This year, however, there would be no tied World Championship, with the Browns taking the title four games to two. Due to injuries and fatigue, Chicago used position players to pitch Game 5, losing 10-3. During the regular season, a May 31 game at the Polo Grounds saw the first crowd of 20,000 in MLB history, witnessing a 4-1 Giants' loss against Detroit.

Hall of Famers Ty Cobb, Rube Marquard, John "Home Run" Baker, and Bill McKechnie were all born in 1886. Cobb, one of baseball's legends, recorded 4,189 hits and 897 stolen bases in his career; his .366 batting average is the best of all time. Marquard led the NL in wins in 1912, the highlight of his eighteen-season Hall of Fame career. Baker, known for his home runs (hence the nickname), led the AL in the category in four consecutive seasons. McKechnie, a Hall of Fame manager, won the World Series with the Reds in 1940.

Connie Mack, Silver King, Mike Smith, Elton "Ice Box" Chamberlain, and Matt Kilroy debuted in 1886. Mack, known for his managerial career, also racked up 659 hits. King debuted at eighteen and won 45 games at age twenty as part of his decade-long career. Smith, also eighteen in 1886, won the AA's ERA title in the following year before turning into an outfielder in the 1890s. Chamberlain totaled 30.7 WAR in his career and has one of baseball's greatest nicknames; you can't put a number on that. Kilroy tossed an MLB-best 66 complete games in both 1886 and 1887, while striking out a record number of hitters.

Will White and Joe Start both played their final games in 1886. White won 40 games in back-to-back seasons and ranks top-twenty all time with his 2.28 ERA and 394 complete games. Start was the only player in the history of the National Association (1871-75) to have at least 200 plate appearances in his National Association career and not be struck out once; he had 1,324 plate appearances for the New York Mutuals from 1871 to 1875 and zero strikeouts.

Philadelphia Quakers via Wikimedia Commons

Interesting numbers from the 1886 season:
- Cap Anson's 147 runs batted in easily became a single-season MLB record, but it would only last for one season. It is currently the third most RBI in a season by someone with 125 games played or fewer.
- Metropolitans first baseman Dave Orr set a record with 193 hits in a season. He also became the first player in MLB history to record 300 total bases in a single season.
- Dave Orr's 31 triples in 1886 made him the first player to reach 30 three-base hits in a season; only two players have

joined him since. To this day, his 31 triples remains the most in a season by a right-handed hitter.

- Dan Brouthers' 40 double, 15 triple, 11 home run season made him the first player in MLB history with a 40/10/10 season. As of the writing of this book, the last player to have a 40/10/10 season was Stephen Drew in 2008. In addition, Brouthers became the first player with multiple 40 double seasons in a career.

- As mentioned earlier, 1886 was the first season where stolen bases were recorded as a statistic. Harry Stovey led the league with 68, and kept his Home Run crown (57 in his career at the end of the season). Not counting National Association records, Stovey became the only player to have the most career home runs and stolen bases at the end of a season.

- On July 5, Fred Carroll set an MLB record with nine hits in a doubleheader. The catcher/first baseman/outfielder had a career high 140 hits in total in the 1886 season for the Alleghenys.

- George Gore became the first player in MLB history to draw 100 walks in a season. Gore is one of two center fielders (Billy Hamilton three times in the 1890s) with 150 runs and 100 walks in a season.

- Bid McPhee set a Reds franchise record by scoring 139 runs in a season. It is the oldest franchise run record that is still standing.

- A year after winning an AA-best 40 games, Bob Caruthers went 30-14, completing 42 of his 43 starts and posting a 2.32 ERA (147 ERA+). He also led the American Association with a .448 on-base percentage and .974 OPS; his 201 OPS+ is the best by a pitcher in a season in MLB history. Caruthers qualifies as a pitcher as more than 50% of his games were on the mound; he played in 44 games as a pitcher and 43 as an outfielder. His two-way season netted him 11.5 WAR.

- The second best seasonal OPS+ by a pitcher also came in 1886. Guy Hecker, a pitcher, first baseman, and outfielder, won the batting title at .341 and also went 26-23 on the mound with a 2.87 ERA. He had a 161 OPS+ and 126 ERA+, making him way above average at both. He totaled 6.0 WAR between pitching and hitting. Hecker is recognized as the only pitcher to win the batting title.
- The top two all-time MLB single-season strikeout totals were set in 1886. Louisville's Toad Ramsey's 499 is the second most in a season ever, but he didn't even lead the American Association in strikeouts. That honor belonged to Pittsburgh rookie Matt Kilroy, who struck out 513 batters over the course of his 1886 campaign.
- Each of the top seven seasons in MLB history in terms of strikeouts belongs to a pitcher from either 1884 or 1886. Eighth place belongs to Nolan Ryan and his 383 punchouts for the California Angels in 1973.
- Matt Kilroy averaged 7.9 strikeouts per 9 innings pitched in his record setting season. The MLB average in 2018 was 8.5 strikeouts per 9 innings pitched. He was able to obtain such a high strikeout total despite that rate due to his MLB leading 588.2 innings pitched. Despite the strikeout records, Kilroy led the league with 34 losses for the Orioles.
- Ed Morris set the Pirates single-season franchise record for strikeouts, with his 326 punchouts for the Pittsburgh Alleghenys in 1886. Morris' 298 strikeouts from the season before still ranks second for the Pirates franchise.
- Toad Ramsey became the first pitcher to issue 200 walks in a season. Ramsey's 207 walks in 1886 would remain a single-

season record until 1889, the first season in which a free pass was awarded after only four balls.

1886 will forever be known for the only 500 strikeout season that baseball will ever see, thanks to the then-recently lifted restrictions on overhand pitching deliveries. Also, 1886 was unofficially dubbed by us, the authors of this book, as the Year of the Pitcher (Who Raked). Following the 1886 season, the NL and AA agreed to create the following rules applying to both leagues: five balls for a walk, four strikes for a strikeout, the creation of a strike zone from shoulders to knees, and a pitching distance of 55 feet, six inches.

1887

Following their second place AA finish, the Pittsburgh Alleghenys were admitted into the National League, replacing the short-lived Kansas City Cowboys. Taking Pittsburgh's place in the American Association? The Cleveland Blues. Additionally, the St. Louis Maroons were sold to a group in Indianapolis for $12,000, they would play the next two seasons as the Indianapolis Hoosiers. The Detroit Wolverines (79-45) and St. Louis Browns (95-40) would square off in a best of 15 World's Series that was played in ten cities. Detroit won the series ten games to five, clinching in game 11 but finishing the 15 game series anyways. Wolverines players Jack Rowe and Sam Thompson combined for 42 hits and 20 runs in the series. In the 1887 season, walks counted as base hits, so all batting average totals mentioned below have removed the player's walk total from the calculation.

Eddie Collins, Shoeless Joe Jackson, Walter Johnson, Grover Cleveland "Pete" Alexander, Harry Hooper, and Joe McCarthy were all born in 1887. Collins played in parts of 25 seasons and racked up 3,315 hits, while Jackson's promising career ended due to scandal after his age-32 season. Johnson and Alexander, perhaps two of the greatest to throw a pitch in MLB history, combined for 790 wins, six Triple Crowns, and ten ERA titles. All but Jackson would eventually become inducted into the Hall of

Fame. Hooper won four World Series titles with the Red Sox in the 1910s, while McCarthy would manage the Yankees to seven championships from 1932 to 1943.

Lave Cross, Mike Tiernan, George Van Haltren, Mike Griffin, Ed McKean, and Gus Weyhing all made their debuts in 1887. Cross, a catcher that'd later become a third baseman, played for over 20 years in the Majors. Tiernan would win two home run titles and back-to-back championships before turning 25. Griffin scored 152 runs for the Orioles in 1889, while Weyhing won 177 games in his first six seasons (at least 26 in each).

Jim McCormick, Bobby Mathews, Larry Corcoran, Hugh Daily, and Charlie Ferguson all played their final games in 1887. Not only did he pitch, but McCormick also played over 50 games in the outfield in his career. Mathews, a prominent National Association pitcher, played for eight different clubs in his 15 year pro-career (including the NA). Corcoran tossed exactly 100 complete games in his first two seasons, and had 256 in his career. "One Arm" Daily recorded 483 strikeouts in the UA in 1884. Ferguson racked up 31.6 WAR in his four career seasons; he had a 120 ERA+ in 1514.2 IP and a 124 OPS+ in 1,078 plate appearances, and some believe he would've become an all-time great had he not contracted typhoid fever.

Interesting numbers from the 1887 season:
- Tip O'Neill led baseball in seemingly every offensive category, putting together one of the most dominant seasons in MLB history. His 167 runs, 225 hits, 52 doubles, .435 batting average, .490 on-base percentage, and .691 slugging percentage were not only all league leaders... they were all new single-

season MLB records. He also led the American Association in triples (19), home runs (14), and runs batted in (123). He is still the only player in MLB history to lead his league in doubles, triples, and home runs in the same season.

- O'Neill also hit for the cycle twice in a five game span. He is one of five players (also John Reilly, Babe Herman, Aaron Hill, Christian Yelich) to hit for multiple cycles in a single season.
- O'Neill's .435 batting average and 167 runs scored are Cardinals franchise records that still stand today. His teammate Arlie Latham scored 163 runs, the second most by a player in Redbirds history.
- The 1.180 OPS posted by O'Neill, who was born in Ontario, is the best by a Canadian player in MLB history. The only other Canada-born players with a 1.000 OPS in a season are Larry Walker and Joey Votto. His 225 hits also leads all Canadians; Walker is the only other one with at least 200. O'Neill would be part of the Canadian Baseball Hall of Fame's inaugural class in 1983.
- Sam Thompson drove in 166 runs, a record that would not be broken until 1921 by Babe Ruth. He is the only player in MLB history with 160 RBI in a season with fewer than 130 games played, and he managed to do it twice (also in 1895). Over the course of his career, Thompson averaged 150 RBI per 162 games, the highest rate in MLB history, just edging out Lou Gehrig (149) and Hank Greenberg (148).
- King Kelly and Ezra Sutton of the Boston Beaneaters set a teammate record by combining to score twelve runs in an August game. To put that in perspective, of the 162 games that the Oakland Athletics played in 2017, none involved their team scoring 12 runs.
- Cincinnati outfielder Hugh Nicol stole 138 bases in 1887,

which remains an MLB record. It's important to note, however, that back then, taking an extra base on a hit (such as going first to third on a single) counted as a stolen base. Three of the top five seasons in terms of stolen bases occurred in 1887:

```
Hugh Nicol 1887 (138)
Rickey Henderson 1982 (130)
Arlie Latham 1887 (129)
Lou Brock 1974 (118)
Charlie Comiskey 1887 (117)
```

- Phillies right fielder Jim Fogarty stole 102 bases and also added eight home runs at the plate. The only player in MLB history with more of both in a season is Rickey Henderson, who hit ten homers and stole 130 bases in 1982 and followed it up with nine and 108 in 1983.
- A year after going 30-9 with a 1.98 ERA, Charlie Ferguson batted .337 in what would tragically be his final season.
- Remember John Ward, the guy who led the NL in wins and strikeouts as a nineteen-year-old in 1879? He hurt his arm, so he moved to the outfield, and then shortstop. He stole 111 bases and batted .338 in 1887.
- Matt Kilroy followed up his record 513 strikeout rookie season with a baseball-leading 46 wins. He only struck out 217 batters this time around, though.
- Phenomenal Smith and Matt Kilroy of the Baltimore Orioles became the first pair of lefties to pitch in 50+ games in the same season for the same team. In fact, their 1887 season was the only time in the first 90 years of professional baseball that

that had ever happened.

- Mike Morrison of the Cleveland Blues walked 205 batters in 1887, a rookie record that has never been topped, and his 1.863 WHIP is the highest of any pitcher who has won at least ten games in a season.
- There have been three pitchers to walk sixteen batters in a game. Two of them (Bill George of New York, George Van Haltren of Chicago) occurred within a month of each other in 1887. Van Haltren, then a rookie, would move to the outfield and collect over 2,500 hits in his career.

Most known for Tip O'Neill's all-time season, which combined contact and power in a way that had not been done before, 1887 also saw historic stolen base numbers, the births of several legends, and a Championship Series spanning fifteen games and ten large American cities.

1888

The American Association replaced the New York Metropolitans (who were purchased by the Brooklyn Grays at the end of the 1887 season) with the Kansas City Cowboys. The Brooklyn Grays made a name change and would go by the Brooklyn Bridegrooms for the next three years. The St. Louis Browns (92-43) completed the season atop of the AA standings for the fourth consecutive year and would meet up with first time champions of the National League, the New York Giants (84-47), in an exhibition World Series. The Giants would win the 1888 World Series six games to four. Fred Dunlap signed a $5,000 contract with the Pittsburgh Alleghenys. Combined with his contract came a $2,000 bonus, making him the highest paid player to date.

Tris Speaker, Ben Taylor, Red Faber, and Zack Wheat were born in 1888. Speaker's 792 doubles would go down as the most in MLB history. Taylor would go into the Hall of Fame after a prominent playing and managing career in the Negro League. Faber would go on to win multiple ERA titles, while Wheat would win a batting title himself.

Charlie Ferguson, of the Philadelphia Quakers, passed away from typhoid fever on April 29th, shortly after his 25th birthday. We're going to give him a little extra space in this section; he deserves it. Ferguson was a super utility player if there ever was one. In his four seasons, he made appearances as a pitcher (183 times), a right fielder (eighteen), a center fielder (22), a left fielder (thirteen), a second baseman (27), and a third baseman (five). He'd finish his short career with a 99-64 W-L record and a 2.67 ERA in 1,514.2 IP, good enough for a 120 ERA+. Ferguson also slashed .288/.364/.372 at the dish, giving him a 124 OPS+ for his career. Ferguson was pretty much a 19th century Shohei Ohtani and Ben Zobrist hybrid with the value of the first four seasons of Freddie Freeman's and Masahiro Tanaka's careers.

Making their Major League debuts in 1888 were Ed Delahanty, Billy Hamilton, Jake Beckley, Hugh Duffy, and Cupid Childs. It would be a few years, but Delahanty would find himself as one of the game's best hitters. Hamilton, a different Billy Hamilton than the active one, happened to be a similar player; the outfielder had four seasons with 100 stolen bases. Beckley totaled 2,938 hits in his career, but never once led his league in the category. Duffy would be most known for the batting average record he would set in 1894, while Cupid Childs not only had a cool name, but also had a solid career, racking up 44.3 WAR.

George Bradley, the first pitcher to lead the National League in ERA, would play in his final game. Third baseman Ezra Sutton would finish an eighteen-year career in which he had appeared in the first National Association and National League games ever played; unfortunately, he landed on the losing side of both of those matchups. Also playing in his final game was Charley Jones, the all-time home run leader on two separate occasions.

Interesting numbers from the 1888 season:

- Rookie William Hoy's 82 stolen bases in 1888 were a new rookie record for the National League. It's a record he would possess for nearly a century. In 1985, the St. Louis Cardinals' Vince Coleman would swipe 110 bases on his way to surpassing Hoy. As of 2018, Hoy's 82 stolen bases in 1888 remains the second-most by a NL rookie in the league's 143 years of existence. The most amazing part of Hoy's story is that he was deaf and mute. He would have to look towards his third base coach for signals so that he knew if a pitch was called a ball or a strike. He is believed to be the reason that umpires began using hand signals to accompany their calls.
- With 33 doubles, 11 triples, and 9 home runs on the year, Dan Brouthers had now put up his sixth consecutive season with 50 or more extra base hits. It's a feat that wouldn't be outdone until Hall of Famer Sam Crawford's nine straight seasons of 50+ XBH for the Detroit Tigers from 1907 to 1915. The next first baseman that would string together six such seasons would be Jim Bottomley of the St. Louis Cardinals; he would put up eight seasons of 50 XBH from 1923 to 1930.
- Dad Clarke, a Cubs pitcher, became the first player in MLB history with more home runs than singles in a season. He had one homer and no singles. For good measure, Clarke's only other hit was a triple.
- The Washington Nationals' .208 team batting average is the worst by a team in National League history. Outfielder Paul Hines led the team by hitting .312; the rest of the team hit a not-too-great .196.
- A league-wide batting average of .239 in 1888 was a steep drop from the .271 BA posted just a season earlier. In fact, the only season on record with a lower batting average is the 1968 season, which is commonly referred to as "The Year of

the Pitcher".

- Tim Keefe finished the year with 335 strikeouts and a 1.34 ERA on his way to a 35-12 record, becoming the fourth pitcher to win the Pitching Triple Crown. He joined Tommy Bond (1877 NL), Old Hoss Radbourn (1884 NL), and Guy Hecker (1884 AA) on that list. Keefe also became the all-time leader in strikeouts, finishing the 1888 season with six short of 2,000. He'd add another 570 strikeouts to his career total before playing in his last game in 1893. Keefe would remain at the top of the career strikeout list for 20 years, until a guy named Cy Young would claim that spot.

- Teammates with 40+ starts and a sub-2.00 ERA in the same season:

```
Tim Keefe/Mickey Welch (1885)
Tim Keefe/Mickey Welch (1888)
```

- Pud Galvin became the first pitcher to total 5,000 career innings pitched. Only twelve other players in history have reached that mark and every one of them has a plaque in Cooperstown. Tim Keefe, Kid Nichols, Cy Young, Walter Johnson, Grover Cleveland Alexander, Warren Spahn, Gaylord Perry, Phil Niekro, Steve Carlton, Don Sutton, Nolan Ryan, and Greg Maddux are the others. These thirteen pitchers account for 1.84% of all the innings pitched from 1876 to 2018. Galvin also became the first 300-game winner in Major League history during the 1888 season.

In 1888, we saw a 300-game winner for the first time. 23 of the

24 members of the 300-win club are in the Hall of Fame, leaving Roger Clemens as the only one on the outside looking in. A new strikeout king was crowned. The St. Louis Browns (now known as the Cardinals) set an unmatched franchise record by finishing atop the standings for the fourth straight season. Upon the conclusion of the 1888 season, the Joint Rules Committee elected to go with a four-ball walk, setting up 1889 to be the first season in which a full count would be three balls and two strikes.

1889

Following the collapse of the Detroit Wolverines, the Cleveland Spiders (formerly the Blues) took their place in the National League. In the AA, the Columbus Salons replaced Cleveland. The Blues/Spiders joined the Pittsburgh Alleghenys (from a few years prior) as American Association teams to hop to the NL. In the National League, the New York Giants (83-43) edged out the Boston Beaneaters (83-45) for the pennant; the Brooklyn Bridegrooms (93-44) did the same in the American Association over the St. Louis Browns (90-45). Louisville finished with by far the worst record in baseball, at 27-111. They are one of three teams in MLB history with at least 100 games played to finish with a winning percentage below .200. The Giants prevailed six games to three over Brooklyn in the World's Series.

Stan Coveleski, Heinie Groh, Wally Schang, and George Burns were all born in 1889. Coveleski would win a World Series and multiple ERA titles in his career, while Groh would win multiple championships to go with back-to-back OBP titles. Schang won a trio of World Series titles, as he was the catcher on the Yankees in the early 1920s. Burns only won one (1921), but won a couple of stolen base titles to go with five run titles.

Pitchers Amos Rusie, Jack Stivetts, Sadie McMahon, and shortstop Herman Long made their debuts in 1889. Rusie, only eighteen years old, started 22 games and closed eleven for the Hoosiers in his rookie year. Stivetts won the AA ERA title in his debut season, leading the way with a 2.25 mark. McMahon would win 85 games in his first three seasons. Herman Long, who played most of his career with Boston, led baseball with a dozen home runs in 1900.

Brooklyn Bridegrooms via Wikimedia Commons

Interesting numbers from the 1889 season:
- Outfielder Harry Stovey totaled 38 doubles, 19 homers, and 63 stolen bases in 1889. He is the only player in MLB history to reach each of those marks in a single season. Stovey also led the American Association in SLG at .525 and tied for the league lead in runs scored (152).
- Orioles outfielder Joe Dowie collected only seventeen hits in

his short-lived Major League career. Five of them, however, came in one game on July 24. Robin Yount, who had 3,142 hits in his Hall of Fame career, also had one career five hit game.

- Tommy Tucker got hit by 33 pitches. He became the first player in MLB history with 30 HBP in a season and also holds the record for most hit by pitches in a player's first six seasons, with 160.

- Harry Stovey of the Philadelphia Athletics once again retook his home run crown, finishing the season with 89 career homers. He wouldn't surrender that title until 1895.

- Mike Griffin of the Baltimore Orioles tied Harry Stovey for the Major League lead in runs scored in 1889 with 152 runs. He managed to reach his total despite going a mere 148-for-531 (.279 BA) at the dish on the season. Griffin's 152 runs scored are the most by a player who had fewer hits than runs scored in a season, and they're also the most runs by a player who carried a sub-.300 batting average for the year.

- Mike Tiernan's 147 runs scored in 1889 are a Giants single-season franchise record. In fact, Tiernan is one of only two Giants to ever have four seasons with at least 125 runs scored. Barry Bonds is the other.

- Bob Caruthers, a Brooklyn pitcher, went 40-11 in 1889. His eleven losses are tied for the fewest among pitchers with 40 wins in a season (Mickey Welch 1885). In '85, Caruthers went 40-13 for the St. Louis Browns. He would finish his career with a record of 218-99, making him the winningest pitcher in MLB history with fewer than 100 losses (unless you count Albert Spalding's National Association career).

- John Clarkson put up a career high 16.7 WAR. He is one of two pitchers in MLB history with three seasons of a dozen pitching WAR. They named a pretty important award after the other guy. Clarkson threw 620 innings in 1889, but would only crack 400 IP once more in his career.

- George Keefe set an MLB record by walking seven batters in one inning during a May 1 game against the Giants. He walked 143 men in 27 starts over the course of the season. This could be a result of the new count rule that reduced the number of balls needed for a walk down to four balls.

- Mark Baldwin of the Columbus Solons set a new MLB record with 83 wild pitches in a season. That's more wild pitches than Grover Cleveland Alexander, Warren Spahn, or Greg Maddux had in their *careers*. Each one of those Hall of Famers finished with over 5,000 innings pitched in their careers.

- From May 22nd through June 22nd, the Louisville Colonels lost 26 consecutive games, a Major League record that still stands today. The streak included an 0-for-21 road trip and a dozen losses that were decided by two or fewer runs.

To be honest, 1889 was a relatively boring year in baseball. The title of Home Run King once again switched hands, and the Louisville Colonels had an all-time awful season.

1890

Six of the National League's eight franchises remained the same from 1889, and a couple of teams got new names...

The Chicago White Stockings became the Chicago Colts, and the Philadelphia Quakers became the "Phillies," a nickname that'd remain with the club for, well, until now. Additionally, the Indianapolis Hoosiers were replaced with another modern team: the Cincinnati Reds, formerly the American Association's Red Stockings, while the Washington Nationals would be replaced by the AA's Brooklyn Bridegrooms. All but two NL teams (Brooklyn and Cleveland) would see their teams last until the publishing of this book. The American Association saw even more change. The league saw an increase to nine teams, four of which were new due to the departure of three teams (the Kansas City Stars were no longer in the AA) and the addition of one. The Toledo Maumees, Rochester Broncos, Syracuse Stars, and Brooklyn Gladiators all made their debut seasons in the American Association.

That's not all! A new Major League, called the "Players National League of Professional Base Ball Clubs", created by John Montgomery Ward (the guy who made the first union), was founded and featured several stars from other leagues. The Players League and National League did not get along. Most notably, the National League and Players League did not want to release their schedules because they were afraid the other would schedule conflicting games, and the NL even released a fake schedule. Both leagues buffed their attendance numbers in order to make it look as if business was going well, despite many games being directly conflicting with the other league. The eight teams in the Players League, in order of their finish in the standings in 1890: the Boston Reds, Brooklyn Ward's Wonders, New York Giants (a different one), Chicago Pirates, Philadelphia Athletics (a different one), Pittsburgh Burghers, Cleveland Infants, and Buffalo Bisons. In the World's Series, the NL champion Brooklyn Bridegrooms tied the AA champion Louisville Colonels, 3-3-1, and both declined to play the PL's Boston Reds in an inter-league playoff.

Max Carey, Sam Rice, Ken Williams, Stuffy McInnis, Casey Stengel, Urban Shocker, Bob Shawkey, and Dolf Luque were born in 1890. Carey is one of two players in MLB history to win ten stolen base titles (also Rickey Henderson). Rice's six 200-hit seasons after turning 30 are tied for the second most in MLB history with Bill Terry; they trail only Ichiro's seven. McInnis was part of a World Series team for three different franchises (Athletics, Red Sox, Pirates), but had only a .477 OPS during his postseason career. Stengel would win an on-base percentage title before becoming a seven time World Series-winning manager for the Yankees from 1949 to 1960. Shocker went 18-6 for the '27 Yankees, while Shawkey went 2-3 for the same team. The duo combined for over 100 WAR in their careers. Luque would pitch in parts of 20 seasons, his best coming in 1923 in which he went 27-8 with a 201 ERA+.

Cy Young, Kid Nichols, George Davis, Jesse Burkett, and Bill Joyce all debuted in 1890. Connie Mack made his managerial debut as well. Cy Young won and lost the most games in MLB history; he pitched in a lot of baseball games. Nichols would lead baseball in wins for three consecutive seasons, and is the only pitcher in MLB history with 25+ wins in each of his first nine seasons. Davis had seventeen seasons with 20+ stolen bases; only Rickey and Honus have had more. Burkett would rack up 2,850 career hits, including 240 in 1896. Joyce's .435 career OBP is the seventh best in MLB history.

Ned Williamson, Jim Whitney, Ed Morris, Guy Hecker, and future HOFer Deacon White would all play their final games in 1890. Ned Williamson is one of five players, along with George Hall, Babe Ruth, Roger Maris, and Barry Bonds, to retire with the single-season home run record. Whitney, as a rookie, led the Majors in both wins and losses; he'd retire at 191-204. Despite only playing seven seasons, Morris reached 38.4 WAR and 1,217 strikeouts. Hecker, who is ineligible for the Hall of Fame because he does not meet the ten-season minimum, famously won a Pitching Triple Crown and then a batting title a couple of years later. Deacon White, brother of Will, was somehow better, playing for twenty years including his National Association days. Per 162 games, he averaged 215 base hits, but the short schedules of the 1870s and 80s prevented his career total from getting much past 2,000.

Interesting numbers from the 1890 season:
- On May 31st, the New York Giants became the first team to hit back-to-back-to-back home runs. They would still end up falling to the Cincinnati Reds by a score of 12-8.
- Harry Stovey made history, becoming the first member of the 100 home run club. The only other player to be the first

to a hundred home run milestone is Babe Ruth, who was the first to 200, 300, 400, 500, 600, and 700 home runs.

- Harley Richardson, of Boston's PL team, became the first and only player to date in MLB history with 150 RBI and 40 stolen bases in a season.

- Richardson also had the first of eight player seasons with 150 runs batted in and zero hit by pitches. It would later be done by Babe Ruth, Jimmie Foxx, Lou Gehrig, Jimmie Foxx again, Hank Greenberg, Jimmie Foxx again, and Vern Stephens.

- Bill Joyce's 123 walks are the second most by a rookie in MLB history behind Aaron Judge's 127 in 2017. Joyce played for Brooklyn's Players' League team, and managed a .413 on-base percentage that year. His career .435 OBP ranks seventh-best all time, one spot behind Barry Bonds (.444) and one spot ahead of Rogers Hornsby (.434).

- Yank Robinson's 72 hits for the Pittsburgh Burghers are the fewest in a season by a Major Leaguer that finished the year with 100+ walks. Robinson slashed .229/.436/.280 in 101 games played in 1890.

- Hub Collins' 148 runs scored are the most in a single season in Dodgers franchise history.

- Mike Griffin scored 127 runs for the Philadelphia Athletics and became the first player to score 500+ runs during his first four years in the Majors. Only four players in history have since done that: Ted Williams (541 runs), Mike Griffin (524), Joe DiMaggio (520), and Albert Pujols (500).

- As a sixteen-year-old in the Players' League, Willie McGill went 11-9 with a 4.12 ERA in 24 games pitched (20 starts).

- In his debut season, Cy Young went 9-7 in sixteen starts. In addition to wins and losses, Young would go on to become MLB's career leader in starts, complete games, innings pitched, hits allowed, earned runs allowed, and batters faced.

- Jack Stivetts struck out 289 hitters for the St. Louis Browns in 1890, setting a Cardinals franchise record that has lasted through at least the 2018 season.

- Toad Ramsey also racked up quite a few strikeout victims for the Browns in 1890. His 257 strikeouts are the ninth-most in Cardinals franchise history. Ramsey and Stivetts became the sixth set of teammates to rack up 250+ strikeouts in the same season. Baseball would have to wait another 73 years to witness the next duo (Don Drysdale and Sandy Koufax) to accomplish this feat.

- Guy Hecker had fewer wins and a worse ERA+ than the year before for the sixth consecutive season. His 2-9 record and 65 ERA+ were career lows, prompting his retirement following his age-34 season.

- In 548.2 innings, nineteen-year-old Giants starter Amos Rusie walked a Major League record 289 batters during the 1890 season, a record that is sure to stay intact until the end of time. In a completely unfair comparison, Greg Maddux walked only 278 opposing hitters in his first eight seasons with Atlanta, spanning 259 starts and 1,876.0 innings pitched.

- The Pittsburgh Alleghenys finished last in the National League with a 23-113 (.169) record. They were outscored by 638 runs for the 1890 season— an average of 4.69 runs per game. Not per loss, but per game! Their pitching staff finished the season with a 56 ERA+, the worst mark for a team in the history of professional baseball.

The Players League only lasted for one season, but its legacy was seen for years. Of note was the creation of several new ballparks, including a new Polo Grounds. In 1968, commissioner William

Eckert declared the PL an official Major League. Additionally, baseball saw the 100 home run club's first member, the debut of Cy Young, and the Majors' first string of three home runs in a row.

1891

The National League returned the same eight teams from the season before, but with a couple of name changes. Brooklyn shortened up their name from the Bridegrooms to the Grooms and Pittsburgh would make its only name change in franchise history, becoming the Pirates that we see in the standings today. The American Association would make a few team changes prior to their 10th and final season. The Broncos, Maumees, and Stars were now out of the AA, and they were replaced by the Boston Reds, Cincinnati Kelly's Killers, and the Washington Statesmen. The Kelly's Killers would fold in August and the Milwaukee Brewers of the Western Association would finish out their schedule. The Boston Beaneaters would finish the season with an 87-51 record, this would be the franchise's 4th NL title and their first in 8 years. The Boston Reds (93-42) were crowned champions in the AA, finishing 8.5 games ahead of the St. Louis Browns.

Like all other years, there were many future ballplayers born in 1891. Some of the most notable of those births include Dazzy Vance, Carl Mays, Eppa Rixey, Dave Bancroft, Rabbit Maranville, Roger Peckinpaugh, and Ray Chapman. Vance would be an elite starter for the Dodgers, winning several consecutive strikeout titles, while Mays would be a front-end starter for several pennant-winning teams. Rixey would play 21 seasons in the National League, winning 266 games despite serving a year in World War I in the heart of his prime. Bancroft, Maranville, and Peckinpaugh would all go on to be elite defensive shortstops. Chapman, a career Indian, would be most known for his tragic death at the hands of a Mays fastball.

Pitching greats Jim Whitney and Larry Corcoran would both die in their early 30s. Whitney had played a year earlier while Corcoran had last pitched in 1887.

Clark Griffith, Hughie Jennings, Joe Kelley, and John McGraw all made their debuts in 1891, beginning their journeys towards Cooperstown. Griffith, a pitcher, would rack up at least eight WAR multiple times in his career, one coming as soon as 1895. Jennings would be most known for getting beaned; he drew 202 hit by pitches from 1894 to 1898. Kelley would steal 443 bases in his career, including a league-leading 87 in 1896. McGraw would record a .466 on-base percentage in his career and also led the Giants to ten NL pennants as a manager. Also making their first appearances were Bill Dahlen (75.4 WAR) and Theo Breitenstein (50.5 WAR), a couple of baseball's most underrated players in the history of the game.

Paul Hines, owner of baseball's first Triple Crown, played in his final game. Also retiring in 1891 was Fred Dunlap; he'll always be best known for owning almost every batting record during the Union Association's one-year history.

Interesting numbers from the 1891 season:

- Tom Brown, an outfielder for the Boston Reds, set a single-season record by scoring 177 runs. Only Billy Hamilton (198 runs in 1894) and Babe Ruth (177 runs in 1921) have ever reached that run total in a season.
- In 1891, Dan Brouthers surpassed Deacon White as the all-time hits leader among left-handed batters. Brouthers would finish his career with 2,303 hits, tying him for the third most hits during the 1800s and the most by any left-hander in the 19th century.
- At twenty years and two months old, Amos Rusie became the youngest pitcher to toss a no-hitter, leading the New York Giants to a 6-0 victory over the Brooklyn Grooms. He broke the record held by his manager, John Montgomery Ward, who was 20 years and 3½ months old at the time of his no-no in June 1880.
- Harry Stovey wrapped up the season with 31 doubles, 20 triples, and 16 home runs in 1891. He became the first of only 12 players to ever put up a 30+ double, 20+ triple, 15+ home run season. Stovey and Hall of Fame outfielder Kiki Cuyler are the only right-handed hitters to accomplish this feat.
- In his first Major League start on October 4th, Theodore Breitenstein tossed a no-hitter against the Louisville Colonels, giving the Browns an 8-0 victory. He's the first of 3 pitchers to throw a no-no in his first start, Bumpus Jones in 1892 and Bobo Holloman in 1953 are the others.
- Browns starter Jack Stivetts followed up his franchise record-setting year of 289 strikeouts with 259 more punchouts. The only other pitcher in Cardinals franchise history with multiple 250 K seasons is Bob Gibson, who did it a staggering

five times.

- John Ewing's 2.27 ERA led the National League in 1891. Ewing is one of only three pitchers to lead the Majors in ERA in his final season. He would be joined by Phil Douglas in 1922 and Sandy Koufax in 1966.
- 1891 saw the top two seasons posted in an unexpected statistic: batters hit by a pitcher. Columbus pitcher Phil Knell plunked 54 guys in his 58 games in 1891, a record which has not come close to being broken since. In fact, the second highest HBP mark by a pitcher was also posted in 1891, by Washington pitcher Frank Foreman. The Statesman pitcher hit 43 batters in 43 games.

With both Boston teams winning their league titles in 1891, an all-Boston World Series should have been played, but it was never to be. The Beaneaters' owners held a season-long grudge against the AA for allowing a second team into the city and refused to meet the Reds in the postseason; it's the first time that there will be no World Series since its creation in 1884. After the season, the American Association was disbanded and the strongest four teams would join the National League for the 1892 season, while the four weakest teams were bought out by the NL for roughly $130,000.

1892

The collapse of the American Association left the National League without a championship opponent. They ended up deciding to split the season in half, with the winner of each half squaring off in the championship. 1892 would be the first 154-game season in MLB's history. Along with the eight National League teams from a year prior, the AA's St. Louis Browns, Baltimore Orioles, Louisville Colonels, and Washington Senators were part of the 1892 NL season. The Boston Beaneaters won the first half of the season, before cutting several players and getting off to a poor start in the second half. Many accused Boston of tanking, as winning the second half would leave them without a team to play in the championship, giving them less revenue due to the lack of the playoff games. The Cleveland Spiders would win the second half of the season, before taking a five game sweep in the championship at the hands of the Beaneaters. Benjamin Harrison became the first president to attend a game while in office, witnessing (presumably) his Senators lose a 7-4 extra inning matchup against Cincinnati.

Ray Schalk, Wilbur Cooper, Sad Sam Jones, Dutch Leonard, Art Nehf, and Bullet Joe Bush were all born in 1892. Schalk, a future Hall of Fame catcher, spent most of his career with the White Sox. Cooper would win over 200 games for Pittsburgh, while Jones would win 229 in his career despite not winning 70 with any one team. Leonard would record an ERA under 1.00 in 1915; Nehf and Bush both pitched at least 15 years and each won a couple of World Series.

Brooklyn outfielder Hub Collins died in the middle of the 1892 season of typhoid fever at age 28. He is one of two players in MLB history with four seasons of 120 runs and 65 stolen bases (also Billy Hamilton).

Willie Keeler, who would collect nearly 3,000 hits in his career despite a 5'4", 140 lb frame, made his debut in 1892.

Many notable players retired in 1892, including Pud Galvin, Mickey Welch, Charlie Buffinton, Hardy Richardson, George Gore, Tip O'Neill, and Ned Hanlon. Galvin retired as the winningest pitcher of all time, with 365 victories to his name. Welch pitched his final decade for the Giants; his 238 wins with the franchise are tied for the third most in franchise history. Buffinton pitched 11 seasons, striking out 1,700 including 417 in 1884. Richardson slugged 73 homers in his career, 62 of which came after he turned 30. Gore, a solid hitter, was the first player to draw 100 walks in a season. O'Neill batted a remarkable .435 in 1887; his .326 career average is the best by a Canada-born player. Hanlon played 13 unremarkable seasons but would eventually win five NL Pennants as a future Hall of Fame manager.

Cleveland Spiders via Wikimedia Commons

Interesting numbers from the 1892 season:

- Topping his record set in 1886, Dan Brouthers' 8.8 WAR season became a new high for a position player, a mark that would stand for over 20 years. Brouthers, 34, hit .335/.432/.480, leading his league in OPS for the eighth and final time in his career. Only Ruth, Hornsby, Cobb, Williams, and Bonds led their league in OPS more times than Brouthers.
- Jack Crooks had one of our favorite seasons of all time from a statistical standpoint. Crooks' .213 average was far from decent, but he had one of the best eyes of any player ever, finishing the year with an outstanding .400 on-base percentage despite the horrid average. He became the only player in MLB history (minimum 500 plate appearances) with more walks than total bases in a single season. He drew 136 free passes to only 131 total bases. His .213/.400/.294 slash

line just seems like a typo, but it was just Jack Crooks being Jack Crooks.

- Crooks would also be the first player to draw an average of more than one walk per game in a season. It wouldn't be done again until Babe Ruth, and as of the writing of this book, the last player to do it was Barry Bonds. Crooks led the league in walks and finished 78th in hits.
- Colonels outfielder Tom Brown became the first player in MLB history to make 500 outs in a season. He had a .227/.284/.285 slash line in 712 plate appearances only a year after leading the AA in hits, runs, stolen bases, and total bases. No player would eclipse Brown's out total of 510 until Woody Jensen, in 1936.
- With 304 strikeouts on the season, Amos Rusie became the first of only three pitchers to strikeout 300+ in three consecutive seasons. Nolan Ryan (1972-1974) and Randy Johnson (1998-2002) are the only others to accomplish this.
- As we saw when he set the walk record in 1890, Amos Rusie didn't just strike out a lot of hitters, but he also issued a lot of free passes. Of the 67 seasons in which a pitcher recorded 300+ strikeouts, here are the lowest strikeout to walk ratios:

```
Amos Rusie (1892) - 1.13 K:BB
Amos Rusie (1890) - 1.18
Amos Rusie (1891) - 1.29
Mark Baldwin (1889) - 1.34
Bill Hutchinson (1892) - 1.65
Nolan Ryan (1977) - 1.67
Nolan Ryan (1976) - 1.79
Nolan Ryan (1974) - 1.82
```

- Cy Young had what would end up being one of the best seasons in his 22-year career. His 36 victories would end up being a career best, and it would be one of the two seasons he led his league in ERA.
- Bill Hutchinson's 314 strikeouts for the Chicago Colts broke the franchise record for strikeouts in a season by just one. The pitcher that he passed for the record was John Clarkson, who struck out 313 hitters for the 1886 Chicago White Stockings. Hutchinson and Clarkson currently have the top four seasons (two apiece) for strikeouts in Cubs franchise history.
- Bumpus Jones tossed a no hitter in his first Major League start on October 15.
- The 1892 Cleveland Spiders are one of just three pitching staffs to have four pitchers with at least a 130 ERA+ and 25 starts in a season. Cy Young (49 GS, 176 ERA+), Nig Cuppy (42 GS, 135 ERA+), John Clarkson (28 GS, 133 ERA+), and George Davies (26 GS, 131 ERA+) would eventually be joined by the 1997 Atlanta Braves and the 2017 Arizona Diamondbacks.

After their first 154 game season, the National League decided to shorten the schedule to 132 games and to abolish 1892's playoff format of first half winner against second half winner. One of our favorite players of all time, Jack Crooks, had one of our favorite seasons of all time, while Dan Brouthers had what was then arguably the best season of all time by a position player.

1893

The National League saw complete league continuity from 1892! All twelve teams who played in the league a year before made a return. Because the National League got rid of its wonky postseason format, there were no playoffs in 1893. The 83-43 Boston Beaneaters were crowned National League champions, finishing five games ahead of the Pittsburgh Pirates. Meanwhile, the Washington Senators' 40-89 record was twelve games worse than the eleventh place Louisville Colonels, easily taking last place in the NL. The pitching mound was moved back to its current distance of 60 feet, six inches from 55 feet, six inches. This vital rule change made 1893 the beginning of baseball's Modern Era.

Hall of Famers George Sisler, Edd Roush, Billy Southworth, Burleigh Grimes, and Jesse Haines were all born in 1893. Sisler would have a historic three season stretch, batting nearly .400 (.39967) from 1920 to 1922. Roush would win two batting titles and a slugging title in his career. Southworth's playing career wasn't special, but he would win a couple of World Series titles as a manager for the Cardinals in the 1940s. Grimes and Haines would both play 19-year careers worthy of Cooperstown inductions.

Lip Pike, the first Jewish player in pro baseball history and National Association home run leader in 1871, '72, and '73, died of heart disease at age 43. We haven't mentioned him much in our book because he hadn't done anything incredible since the founding of the National League, but he was one of the pivotal players in the NA.

Bill Lange and Red Donahue debuted in 1893. Lange would play only seven seasons, but he would still steal a total of 400 bases. Donahue would pitch until 1906, recording at least 6.0 pitching WAR twice.

One of baseball's first true sluggers, Harry Stovey, called it quits following the 1893 season. His 122 career home runs were the most in MLB history at the time of retirement, and he is one of three players in MLB history to average more than one run scored per game in his career (with a minimum of 1,000 games played). In addition to Stovey, King Kelly, Charlie Bennett, Henry Larkin, Tim Keefe, and Bob Caruthers retired. Caruthers led the league in wins, ERA, and OPS at least once each in his career, while Keefe retired with the most WAR of any pitcher to ever take the mound, at 88.8. Kelly scored 519 runs from 1884-1887, leading the NL three times out of those four seasons. Bennett, a catcher, posted a 150 OPS+ in three consecutive seasons, while Larkin led the AA in doubles in two of his first three seasons.

Interesting numbers from the 1893 season:
- Phillies outfielder "Sliding Billy" Hamilton hit .380/.490/.524. Despite only playing 82 games, he managed to qualify for the batting title. Thus, his average topped the NL, and his OBP not only topped the league, but was also a new Major League best, if you look closely. The previous best was Tip O'Neill's .490 in 1887. Rounding to more decimal places, we see that

O'Neill's .48951 fell just short of Hamilton's new mark of .48956. Both round to .490. Without spoiling anything, We'll just say that Hamilton's record did not quite stand the test of time.

- With Hamilton, along with Sam Thompson and Ed Delahanty, Philadelphia had one of the best outfields in MLB history. The trio finished 1-2-3 in the Majors in batting average, and each finished with an OPS+ north of 150. The Phillies as a whole hit .301, and after removing pitchers, their team average comes out to a staggering .315.
- Philadelphia had the NL's leader in position player WAR (Delahanty), batting average and on-base percentage (Hamilton), slugging percentage (Delahanty), plate appearances (Thompson), hits and doubles (Thompson), and home runs and RBI (Delahanty).
- Delahanty also became the second player in MLB history (Hardy Richardson in 1890) with 145 RBI and 35 stolen bases in a season. Since "Big Ed," Hugh Duffy (1894) and Ken Williams (1922) have done the same.
- Our guy Jack Crooks led the league in walks for the second season in a row, with 127. His slash line of .237/.408/.306 is just so… obscure.
- Piggy Ward reached base in seventeen consecutive plate appearances, a mark that would be tied around 70 years later, but never topped.
- Cy Young *led the Majors* with a 0.99 strikeout to walk ratio. He is the only player in baseball history to lead the Majors in K/BB with more walks than strikeouts.
- On August 16, Bill Hawke threw baseball's first no hitter from 60'6".
- Theodore Breitenstein led the Majors with a 3.18 ERA; no

one else has ever led the Majors with an ERA higher than 2.81 (Lefty Grove - 1929).

In baseball's first season with a new pitching distance, baseball saw a drastic increase in offense (from 5.1 runs per team per game in 1892 to an unbelievable 6.6 in 1893, and an increase in batting average from .245 to .280). Harry Wright, manager of the Phillies, began requiring his players to hit a dozen balls prior to each game in 1893; Wright will forever be credited as the originator of batting practice.

1894

As a consequence of the increased mound distance from 1893, 1894 was quite possibly the craziest statistical year in baseball from an offensive perspective. For the second year in a row, the National League did not gain or lose teams, with all twelve remaining the same from a year prior. The Baltimore Orioles' 89-39 record topped the NL, with the New York Giants' 88-44 mark coming second. Baseball's inaugural Temple Cup matched up the two teams in a best of seven series, which New York swept 4-0. Midseason, the Baker Bowl (home of the Phillies) burned down, forcing them to play home games at a local university.

Harry Heilmann, Herb Pennock, Joe Judge, Ford Frick, and George Weiss were born in 1894. Heilmann would win four batting titles in a seven-year span for Detroit in the 1920s. Pennock, a future three-time World Series champion with the Yankees, would go 162-90 with the club. Judge, a Washington Senator for most of his career, ranks third on the Twins career hit list with 2,291 (the Senators would become the Twins). Ford Frick would serve as MLB's third commissioner, while Weiss would serve as Yankees general manager during seven of their World Series winning seasons.

King Kelly and Ned Williamson died in '94. Kelly is the only player in MLB history to play 500 career games at both catcher and right field. Williamson still held the single-season record with 27 home runs at the time of his death.

Bobby Wallace, Fred Clarke, and Jesse Tannehill made their debuts in 1894. Wallace's 2,309 hits would rank 18th all time among shortstops. Clarke, an outfielder, would top him with 2,678 career hits, including four consecutive seasons of at least 180. Tannehill would win an ERA title in 1901.

John Montgomery Ward, Pete Browning, John Clarkson, and Charlie Comiskey played their final games in 1894. Ward led his league in ERA in 1878 as an 18-year-old, wins and strikeouts in 1879, and stolen bases twice later on in his career after transitioning to the outfield. Browning won three batting titles, retiring with a career .341 average. Clarkson was a three time strikeout and win champion, finishing his career with 84.9 pitching WAR. Comiskey would go on to have quite a successful career as owner of the White Sox.

Interesting numbers from the 1894 season:
- On May 11th, Orioles shortstop Hughie Jennings was hit by three pitches in one game, a first in baseball history.
- In their 20-11 victory over Cincinnati on May 30, Boston second baseman Bobby Lowe became the first player in MLB history to hit four home runs in a game. All came off Reds pitcher Ice Box Chamberlain. In his career, he hit 71 home runs in 18 seasons, good for an average of just under four per year.
- Boston right fielder Jimmy Bannon hit grand slams on August 6th and 7th; he became the first to ever hit grand slams on

consecutive days.

- The Boston Beaneaters as a team cracked 103 home runs, joining the 1884 Chicago White Stockings (142 HR) as the only non Live Ball Era teams to hit the triple digit mark for dingers in a season. Boston's home run total was aided by a temporary relocation of home games after the South End Grounds burned down in May. They would move to the homer-friendly Congress Street Grounds for 27 games until the South End Grounds were rebuilt and reopened on July 20th. SABR estimates that the distance from home plate to the fence on the foul lines did not top 250 feet. All four of Bobby Lowe's home runs in his historic game were pulled over the fence down the left field line.

- The Beaneaters also became the second team in MLB history (again, the 1884 White Stockings) to have five players hit double-digit home runs.

- There have been 64 times in Major League history that a player has accumulated 130 runs and 130 RBI in a season. Walt Wilmot became one of those 64 when he scored 136 runs and drove in 130 RBI for the Chicago Colts (Cubs) in 1894, and despite the run production, he still somehow managed to post a below average OPS+ for the season. Wilmot's 97 OPS+ is 34 points lower than the next lowest 130/130 season (Al Simmons' 1932).

- Once again, Philadelphia's bats were outstanding, especially their outfield. Their three main outfielders (Delahanty, Thompson, and Hamilton), along with backup outfielder Tuck Turner, all hit at least .400. Tucker managed 347 at-bats himself. The quartet combined for a batting average of .409.

- The Phillies as a whole batted .350, the best batting average for a team in MLB history. Meanwhile, Baltimore's .418 on-base percentage and .901 OPS were also the best by a team in MLB history. None of the three marks have ever been matched. Since integration in 1947, the best team OBP in a season is .385 by the 1950 Red Sox and the best OPS is .851 by the 2003 Red Sox.

- Remember that OBP record that Billy Hamilton took last season, at .490? That was broken in 1894... by four different players, including Hamilton himself. Hamilton topped the league at .521, with Hugh Duffy (.502), Joe Kelley (.502), and Bill Joyce (.496) all topping the previous single-season best.

- Hamilton reached base safely 362 times, destroying the previous record of 303, set by Cupid Childs in 1892. With regard to reaching base safely, only two other seasons will ever eclipse Hamilton's 1894 season: Babe Ruth's 379 TOB in 1923 and Barry Bonds' 376 TOB in 2004.

- Billy Hamilton crossed home plate 198 times in 132 games. His 198 runs scored in 1894 is still a record today.

- The Phillies center fielder had his fourth season of at least 100 stolen bases in 1894, an MLB record. Hamilton, 28, had already stolen 543 bases in his career.

- In addition to Hamilton, Hugh Duffy (Beaneaters, who eventually became the Braves) and Jake Stenzel (Pirates) set still-standing franchise records in runs scored in a season. Duffy scored 160, while six more teammates each scored at least 110 runs, including 158 from Bobby Lowe. Stenzel's 150 were only three more than teammate Patsy Donovan.

- Finishing his season with 225 hits, Billy Hamilton tied the previous single-season high for hits, set by Tip O'Neill in 1887. His 225 hits would only be good enough for second best in 1894, though. Duffy, the Beaneaters' center fielder, spoiled Hamilton's record-tying season by cracking 237 hits of his own. Duffy would only keep baseball's single-season hits record for a couple years.

- Duffy's .440 batting average became a new single-season best in the Majors, and hasn't since been beaten. He went 237-for-539, meaning he could've gone 0 for his next 250 and still finished the season with a batting average greater than .300.
- Duffy's incredible season also finished with him having the most total bases in a season. His 374 TB would stay atop the leaderboard until 1920, the first year of the Live Ball Era. Duffy's 85 extra base hits were also a record total, tying tied him with Tip O'Neill, who set his record in 1887 for the St. Louis Browns of the American Association. Their record of 85 XBH would stand until Babe Ruth's first season in pinstripes.
- Orioles second baseman Heinie Reitz became the second player ever with 30 triples in a season. He racked up 31 of his 65 career triples in 1894.
- Colts' second baseman Jiggs Parrott had quite possibly the worst offensive season of all time, all things considered. His .605 OPS on the surface isn't awful, but the league average OPS of .814 puts it into perspective. According to Baseball Reference, he was 64 runs worse than the average player with his bat, the worst mark by a player in MLB history. His OPS+ was an abysmal 42.
- With outfielders Willie Keeler and Joe Kelley (165 each) and third baseman John McGraw (156), Baltimore became the first team (and only team) in MLB history to have three players score 150 runs in a season. The aforementioned Reitz only scored 86 runs.
- The top three seasons by a team in terms of OPS occurred in

1894. Baltimore's .901 paces all teams in MLB history, with the Phillies (.893) and Beaneaters (.885) following shortly behind.

- The Boston Beaneaters had seven players score at least 100 runs in 1894. Seven! In fact, all seven of those guys scored 112 or more runs that year with Hugh Duffy's 145 runs leading the way. This Beaneaters team remains the only MLB team to ever have seven players reach the century mark in runs scored in a single season.
- MLB teams to finish a season with a .400+ OBP:

```
1894 Baltimore Orioles (.418)
1894 Philadelphia Phillies (.415)
1894 Boston Beaneaters (.401)
```

- Hall of Famers Dan Brouthers, Hughie Jennings, Willie Keeler, Joe Kelley, John McGraw, and Wilbert Robinson all played in 100+ games for the Baltimore Orioles. The only other teams to have six Hall of Famers play 100+ games in a season were the 1925 Giants (they had seven) and the 1929, 1931, 1932, & 1933 Yankees.
- Despite having only twelve teams, 1894 had 26 players with a .300 batting average and 100 runs batted in, the fifth most all time. The most .300/100 players in a season in the 2010s is 12, set in 2011. 1894 had more than twice that total despite fewer than half of the teams.
- Amos Rusie claimed the Pitching Triple Crown in 1894. Rusie joined Tommy Bond, Old Hoss Radbourn, Tim Keefe, and John Clarkson as the only pitchers to post a Triple Crown season during the 1800s.

- Amos Rusie and Jouett Meekin became the only teammates to be worth 10+ pitching WAR in the same season. Rusie ended the season with 13.7 Pitching WAR and Meekin with 10.8.

1894 saw one of the greatest run explosions that baseball has ever witnessed. While it occurred during the "Dead Ball Era," 1894's numbers are staggering, so far removed from a modern fan's perception of the game that the stats don't even begin to tell the story of the season. Baseball saw its first four home run performance, an outfield full of .400 hitters, and a lineup full of Hall of Famers, to name a few things.

1895

Once again, the same dozen teams remained in the National League for another season. The Baltimore Orioles took the National League Pennant at 87-43, but lost four games to one to the 84-46 Cleveland Spiders in the second year of the Temple Cup. Nine of the twelve teams finished with a record above .500, while the bottom three teams (Washington, St. Louis, Louisville) combined for a 117-273 record, or .300 winning percentage. The gap between the eighth place Giants and ninth place Senators was a whopping 21.5 games.

Pitcher/outfielder/legend Babe Ruth and High Pockets Kelly were born in 1895. Ruth's 714 home runs are currently third-most all time. He also had a 2.28 ERA in over 1,200 innings on the mound. Kelly, also a future Hall of Famer, was part of the Giants team that defeated Ruth's Yankees in consecutive World Series.

Harry Wright, one of the game's pioneers, died of a lung ailment in October of '95. He is also credited with being one of the first to "shift" his team's defense based on where hitters hit the ball the most.

Jimmy Collins, Al Orth, and Harry Davis made their debuts at some point during the 1895 season. Collins would play 1,435

107

career games for Boston teams (741 for the Americans, 674 for the Beaneaters). Orth would walk only 32 hitters in 33 starts in 1901 for the Phillies, while Davis would take home four consecutive AL home run titles with Philadelphia's other team, the Athletics.

Jack Glasscock, who led the NL in hits in 1889 and 1890, and debuted all the way back in 1879, played his final game in 1895.

Interesting numbers from the 1895 season:
- Cap Anson, at 43 years old, became the oldest player in MLB history to reach the 200 total base mark in a season. Since then, the next oldest player to total 200 in a season was 42-year-old Carlton Fisk in 1990.
- Sam Thompson drove in 165 runs in only 119 games, falling an RBI short of the single-season record he set in 1887, when he played 127 games. His OPS was more than 100 points better in 1895 than it was in 1887. The only other players in MLB history with multiple 165 RBI seasons? Gehrig (four such seasons), Foxx, Ruth, and Greenberg.
- Roger Connor overtook Harry Stovey's career home run record. Coming into the season needing four homers to equal the all-time record, Connor's eight was *easily* enough to claim the crown with 126. He would retire with 138 home runs to his name, the most by any player until Babe Ruth would surpass him in 1921.
- Poor Ed Delahanty hit better than .400 for the second season in a row, but once again could not claim the National League's batting title, falling a point short of Jesse Burkett's .405 mark. From 1893 to 1895, Delahanty had a slash line of .391/.465/.594.
- With an OBP of exactly .500 (286 times on base in 572 tries),

Burkett became the third player in two years (Hugh Duffy and Joe Kelley in 1894) with a .500 on-base percentage and more than 45 doubles in a season. Since then, no player has managed to join the trio on that exclusive list.

- Jesse Burkett racked up 185 singles in 1895, a new single-season record. He'd manage to reach at least 185 in three other seasons, making him responsible for four of the thirteen seasons with that many singles. The only other player with four seasons of 185 singles is Ichiro Suzuki, who had a single-season record 225 one baggers in 2004.

- Billy Hamilton followed up his fourth career 100 stolen base season with a 95 steal year. It was his fifth season with at least that many; no other player even has four such seasons. Hamilton is responsible for 5 of the 29 seasons with at least 95 steals.

- Teammates with a .470+ OBP in the same season:

```
        Ed Delahanty and Billy Hamilton
           of the 1894 Philadelphia Phillies
        Ed Delahanty and Billy Hamilton
           of the 1895 Philadelphia Phillies
        Lou Gehrig and Babe Ruth
           of the 1927 New York Yankees
        Lou Gehrig and Babe Ruth
           of the 1930 New York Yankees
```

- Jack Clements put up a 171 OPS+ in 1895; he's just one of four catchers (with at least 50% of games coming at the position) to ever put up that high of a mark. The other catchers to put up at least 170 OPS+ for a season are Mike Piazza (twice), Buster Posey, and Joe Mauer.

- The Louisville Eclipse averaged 5.25 runs per game, which ranked last in baseball. In 2018, only the World Champion Red Sox averaged more than 5.25 runs per game, while the 2018 Yankees averaged that figure exactly.
- Amos Rusie's 201 strikeouts gave him his fifth strikeout title of his career, at only 24 years old. "The Hoosier Thunderbolt," who *supposedly* threw mid-to-upper 90s with his fastball, would only strike out 255 more batters in his entire injury-ridden career that included hearing damage from a line drive that struck him in the head and, more importantly, arm problems. Rusie's 201 strikeouts were more than twice as many as Jack Taylor's 93, which ranked seventh best in the NL.
- Baltimore's Bill Hoffer concluded the 1895 season with a ridiculous 31-6 record. Out of the 941 pitcher seasons in which a National League pitcher started 35+ games, Hoffer's .838 W-L% ranks second behind only Doc Gooden's 1985 season. Gooden posted a 24-4 record in his 35 starts with the New York Mets that year, good enough for a .857 W-L%.

Similar to previous years with the new mound distance, 1895 was a hitter's year. The most amazing feat, in my opinion, was Cap Anson's major league success continuing his success through the beginning and middle of his 40s. From a 19-year-old leading the National Association in doubles in its debut season in 1871 to accumulating 200 total bases in his age 43 season in the NL, Anson's career progression is nothing short of incredible. He still had a couple more campaigns left in him, too.

1896

Aside from the Brooklyn Grooms changing their nickname back to the Bridegrooms, there were once again no changes to the National League's structure from the previous season. Once again, Baltimore and Cleveland finished as the top two teams in the league, this year finishing at 90-39 and 80-48, respectively. Getting revenge on their 1895 defeat, the Orioles swept the Temple Cup in four games.

1896 saw the births of Rogers Hornsby, Jimmy Dykes, Bob Meusel, Tom Zachary, Rube Walberg, and Bucky Harris. Hornsby is one of seven players in MLB history with a 1.000 career OPS. Dykes, a very versatile player, appeared in at least 140 games at each infield position in his career; he'd record 2,256 hits as well. Meusel played all of the 1920s for the Yankees, winning a trio of World Series in his time in New York. Zachary would pitch 19 seasons, and also won a couple of World Series in his career (one for Washington, one for the Yankees). Walberg won back-to-back titles with the Athletics in 1929 and 1930; he'd pitch for 15 seasons. Harris played in a dozen seasons before becoming a Hall of Fame manager.

Curt Welch died at 34 years old. He got hit by 70 pitches from 1890 to 1891.

Nap Lajoie, Fielder Jones, and Cy Seymour made their debuts in the 1896 season. Lajoie would win five batting titles in his career, and a slugging title as soon as the following year. Jones would rack up over 40 WAR in his career despite never reaching the 5.0 mark in a single-season; he consistently placed anywhere from 3.0 to just under 5.0. Seymour would have a historic season in 1905, driving in 121 runs as a result of 219 hits, 69 of which came for extra bases.

Ice Box Chamberlain, Tommy McCarthy, and Connie Mack retired from playing in 1896. Chamberlain was only 28 at the time of his final game, but had won 157 games in his career. McCarthy, probably baseball's worst Hall of Famer, totaled 14.6 WAR in his 13 seasons in the Majors. He was known for his smarts, as many believe he developed the hit-and-run play. Mack would continue managing until 1950!

Interesting numbers from the 1896 season:
- Jesse Burkett led the National League in hits for the second straight season. His 240 hits in 1896 became a new single-season record. 191 of those went for singles, surpassing the single-season record of 185 singles he set the year before. Despite batting .410, Burkett *only* had a slugging percentage of .541 due to his relatively low extra base hit total. Burkett had an isolated power of only .131, meaning he averaged only 0.131 extra bases per at bat.
- On July 13th, Ed Delahanty became just the second person to ever hit four home runs in a game. Delahanty is the only player to ever have an inside-the-park home run as a part of a four homer game; in fact, he hit two inside-the-parkers in

that historic showing.

- Delahanty just missed out on his third consecutive season with a .400 average, finishing the year at a measly .397. Over the last three seasons, the Philadelphia outfielder had a slash line of .402/.483/.611. His .631 slugging percentage in 1896 was a career best.
- Hitters with 20+ HBP and 100+ BB in a season:

```
Bill Joyce (1896)
Jason Giambi (2003)
Prince Fielder (2010)
Shin-Soo Choo (2013)
```

- Hughie Jennings would do whatever he could to find his way on the basepaths, and in 1896, he proved exactly that by setting a still-standing record for times being hit by a pitch. Jennings would end up getting plunked 51 times! That's more HBP's than Hall of Famers Chipper Jones, Eddie Murray, and Harold Baines had in their entire careers... combined!
- We don't have batter vs. pitcher data going back all the way to 1896, but it'd be reasonable to assume that Danny Friend, a Cubs pitcher, plunked Jennings on at least one occasion. Friend's 39 hit by pitches rank as the sixth most by a pitcher in a season in MLB history.
- Along with getting plunked an unreasonable amount of times, Jennings also batted .401 and stole 70 bases. The shortstop led the Majors in both offensive and defensive WAR in 1896.
- William Hoy laid down 33 sacrifices in 1896, a new NL record. To make the comparison to today's game, there were only nine teams in the 2018 season that finished with more than

33 sacrifice hits.

- We don't usually want to shine a light on the hitter who leads the league in strikeouts, but we're going to see if we can shed a positive light on the 1896 leader. Tom McCreery had 58 strikeouts to lead all hitters in the National League that year. Those 58 strikeouts are the lowest amount by a league leader in a season that contained at least 100 games (since 1884). Only Ducky Holmes in 1899 and Babe Ruth in 1918 matched McCreery's total of 58 strikeouts while leading the league. McCreery also led the league with 21 triples.

- Cy Young led the Majors with 140 strikeouts (as a pitcher) in 1896. This ended up being the only season in Young's career that he would lead the Majors in strikeouts despite him having nine other seasons in which he tossed more than 140 strikeouts.

The Baltimore Orioles were crowned champions for the third straight year (note: the Temple Cup was considered an exhibition and technically did not determine a champion). The next three-peat wouldn't happen again until the Yankees won four straight World Series titles from 1936 to 1939. This season would also finish with Amos Rusie, 1894's pitching Triple Crown winner, not throwing a single pitch. Rusie sat out the entire season in protest of a $200 fine from the Giants' owner, he was fined $100 for violating curfew and another $100 for simply not trying hard enough. Rusie hired John Montgomery Ward for representation in court and sued the Giants for $5,000. Eventually they settled outside of court with the National League paying Amos the $5,000, instead of the Giants. Rusie then signed a $3,000 contract to go back and play for the Giants in 1897.

1897

The 90-40 Orioles defeated the 93-39 regular season champion Beaneaters four games to one for their second consecutive Temple Cup victory. This would be the fourth and final Temple Cup played, with Baltimore being the only repeat victor. Every Temple Cup series was either a 4-0 sweep or 4 games to 1.

Frankie Frisch, Ross Youngs, Lefty O'Doul, and Eddie Rommel were born in 1897. Frisch would play for 19 seasons, finishing only 120 hits away from 3,000 in his career. Youngs, despite dying at 30, would rack up 1,491 hits and win multiple World Series. O'Doul would win a couple of batting titles, while Rommel won two win titles.

Charles "Old Hoss" Radbourn, winner of a Major League single-season record 59 wins in 1884, passed away at age 42.

Honus Wagner, Rube Waddell, Jack Powell, Jimmy Sheckard, and Roger Bresnahan all debuted in 1897. Wagner had 81 of his eventual 3,420 career hits in 1897. Waddell would be one of baseball's first true strikeout artists, leading baseball in five consecutive seasons. Powell's 422 complete games in his career would be top-15 all time. Sheckard was an outfielder on the Cubs when they won back-to-back titles; he went 5 for 21 with

2 doubles and a stolen base in both the 1907 and 1908 Series. Bresnahan would be known for his unique transition from catcher to center field back to catcher again.

Cap Anson and Roger Connor retired as career hit and home run kings in 1897, respectively. Anson racked up 3,435 hits while Connor slugged 138 homers. Buck Ewing and Silver King called it quits as well. King won multiple ERA titles while Ewing averaged 200 hits per 162 games over the course of his 18 season career.

Interesting numbers from the 1897 season:
- Willie Keeler easily led the National League with a .424 batting average. He remains one of two qualified players to hit .400 with no home runs (Hughie Jennings in 1896). Keeler's .424 BA, 239 hits, and 145 runs are the most in a season by a player that didn't hit a home run.
- Keeler, over the next five seasons including this one, hit .377 in 2,853 at bats, striking out only twenty times. He struck out five times in '97.
- Keeler also broke Jesse Burkett's record with 193 singles in a season. Burkett had set the record in 1895 with 185 and one-upped himself with 191 in '96.
- The Giants' George Davis became the first shortstop in MLB history with 135 RBI in a season. He would later be joined by only Vern Stephens, Ernie Banks, Álex Rodríguez, and Miguel Tejada.
- Harry Davis (no relation to the aforementioned George Davis) led the National League with 28 triples in 1897, despite finishing tied for 21st with only 40 extra base hits. To this day, he is the only player to have more than 15 extra base hits in a season and have at least 70% of those come via the triple.

- Nap Lajoie, in his first full seasons in the Majors, drove in 127 runs and led the league with a .569 slugging percentage. Lajoie's 127 RBI would end up being a career high despite playing in 19 more seasons after '97.
- Orioles outfielder Jake Stenzel hit 43 doubles, drove in 116 runs, and stole 69 bases. The only other players to go 40/110/60 in a season are Walt Wilmot in 1894 and Ty Cobb in 1911.
- Browns pitcher Red Donahue went 10-35 with a 6.13 ERA. No one has lost 35 in a season since and it's very likely that he will be the final 35 game loser in MLB history. St. Louis went 29-102 that year, so it's not like he was a liability or anything.
- Donahue actually led the Browns pitching staff in wins in '97. Here are the W-L records of every St. Louis pitcher to get a decision in 1897:

```
     10-35
      9-27
      3-8
      2-7
      1-6
      1-5
      1-4
      1-2
      1-2
      0-4
      0-2
```

- The St. Louis Browns' .221 W-L% ranks as the tenth worst in Major League history. Their 85 OPS+ is one point higher than the 1969 Mets, who finished their season with 100 wins and a World Series banner being hung at Shea Stadium. The 1897 Browns finished with a slightly higher team batting average than the 2002 New York Yankees; those Yankees won 103 games. Needless to say the Browns' pitching was their detriment in 1897.

- With his 135 strikeout season, and his final dominant campaign in his career, Amos Rusie had passed the 1,750 career strikeout mark (he had 1,830). The only other pitcher to hit that milestone by his eighth season in the Majors is Tom Seaver, who struck out 1,856 batters from 1967 to 1974.
- Cy Swaim, a 6'6" (198 cm) pitcher for the Washington Senators, made his debut on May 3rd. Swaim tied a nearly thirteen-year-old record for tallest major leaguer, a mark that was set by Anton Falch in September 1884.

Charles Hinton invented the first pitching machine in 1897, and the final Temple Cup series would be played. Rusie's stretch of dominance would come to an end, and Willie Keeler's aversion to strikeouts remains a feat that'll always be unbelievable.

1898

The National League decided to give a 154-game schedule a second shot; the previous attempt came six years earlier and only lasted for the one year. The NL doubled the number of umpires used to officiate a game; there will now be an umpire behind the plate and another in the field. As for the final standings, the Boston Beaneaters would finish with a 102-47 record on their way to winning a second consecutive pennant. The Baltimore Orioles, led by Doc McJames, would wind up six games back of Boston.

There were six Hall of Famers born in 1898: Happy Chandler, Andy Cooper, Kiki Cuyler, Bill Terry, Pie Traynor, and Joe Sewell. Also born in 1898 was Firpo Marberry, considered to be the first great relief pitcher in history. Chandler served as MLB's commissioner from 1945 to 1951, while Cooper never got the chance to play; he did go 116-57 in the Negro Leagues. Cuyler would win back-to-back run titles in the mid-1920s, while Terry would slash .341/.393/.506 in his career, including a .401 average in 1930. Traynor batted at least .300 in ten different seasons, but never won a batting title. Sewell did the same in nine different seasons, and like Traynor, never led the league. Although the stat was unofficial in his day, Marberry led baseball in saves five times.

Charles Byrne, the founder of the Brooklyn ball club that would eventually become the Los Angeles Dodgers of today, passed away at the age of 54. The winning pitcher for the very first game played in the National Association, Bobby Mathews (55.1 career WAR), would also meet his demise in 1898.

The most notable debuts in 1898 include Vic Willis, Elmer Flick, Frank Chance, Tommy Leach, and Sam Leever. Willis went 25-13 with a 2.84 ERA in his first season, and would win the ERA title in his sophomore year. Flick would start his career with ten straight years with 10 triples and 20 stolen bases, making him the only player in MLB history to do such. Chance never played more than 100 games until 1903, when he'd steal an MLB high 67 bases for the Cubs. Leach would play 2,156 games in his career, but didn't make 1,000 appearances at any one position; he played in 955 at third and 998 in center. Leach would become the only player in MLB history to play in 900 games at both third base and center field. Leever would lead the league in winning percentage three times in five years come the turn of the 20th Century.

Bill Joyce retired from the game. Joyce and Ted Williams are still the only players to ever put up 120+ hits, 120+ walks, and 120+ runs in a season prior to their age 23 season.

Interesting numbers from the 1898 season:
- On April 21st, Bill Duggleby became the first player to crack a grand slam in his first career at bat. It's a feat that would go unmatched through the entire 20th century until Jeremy Hermida's pinch-hit grand slam in his Major League debut with the Florida Marlins on August 31st, 2005. The only others to do this are Kevin Kouzmanoff in 2006 and Daniel

Nava in 2010.

- Willie Keeler led the National League with 216 hits, 206 of which were singles. He was the first player in MLB history with 200 singles in a year. 1898 was the sixth year in a row in which the single-season singles record (try saying that three times fast!) was broken.

- As a byproduct of his ridiculous singles rate, Keeler would finish the season with only 230 total bases, good enough for fourteenth-most in 1898. Keeler's 230 total bases are by far the fewest for a player with at least 200 hits in a season. For an extreme comparison, in 2017, Joey Gallo had 241 total bases on only 94 hits. Keeler had 230 TB on 216 hits in 1898. Gallo also struck out 49 times as often, finishing with 196 whiffs to Keeler's four. Keeler was known for his "Hit 'Em Where They Ain't" approach, while Gallo truly took that to heart when he realized that there aren't any defenders past the outfield.

- Orioles' Hughie Jennings was hit by 46 pitches to lead all hitters. His teammate Dan McGann finished the season with 39 hit by pitches, 16 more than the third place finisher, Bill Dahlen. Jennings and McGann are the only pair of teammates in Major League history to be plunked 30+ times in the same season.

- For the ninth time in as many seasons, Kid Nichols won at least 25 games. No other pitcher has won 25+ games in each of their first seven seasons.

- Speaking of 25+ wins in a season. Kid Nichols (31 wins) and his teammates, Ted Lewis (26 wins) and Vic Willis (25 wins) became just the second trio of pitchers to pick up at least 25 winning decisions in the same season. These three hurlers for the Boston Beaneaters joined the 1887 St. Louis Browns as the only teams to ever accomplish this feat.

- Bert Cunningham (28 wins, 34 strikeouts) of the Louisville Colonels and Al Maul (20 wins, 31 strikeouts) of the Baltimore Orioles are the first 20-game winners with less than 40 strikeouts since the debut season of the National League, when Al Spalding and Bobby Mathews both completed this rare feat. In fact, only six pitchers have ever done this. Along with the aforementioned four pitchers, Slim Sallee in 1919 and Sloppy Thurston in 1924 are the two others.

- Only one left-handed Giants pitcher has tossed more strikeouts in a season than Cy Seymour's 239 in 1898. That guy is Madison Bumgarner, who recorded 251 punchouts for the San Francisco Giants in 2016. Seven years later Seymour would win a batting title as a center fielder for the Cincinnati Reds. His 219 hits in 1905 are the second most in a season by a Reds player, behind only Pete Rose's 230 base knocks in 1973.

- On April 22nd, with a full slate of six games on the schedule, there were a pair of no-hitters thrown. Theo Breitenstein picked up his second career no-no in an 11-0 drubbing of the Pittsburgh Pirates. Meanwhile, in Baltimore, Jay Hughes was shutting down Billy Hamilton and the Beaneaters for his only career no-hitter.

- Red Donahue of the Phillies tossed a no-no against Boston in July and the next month the Bridegrooms went hitless against Chicago Orphans' pitcher, Walter Thornton on August 21st. Along with the two no-hitters thrown on April 22nd, this was the first Major League season with more than 3 no-hitters.

- The St. Louis Browns' win-loss record of 39-111 (.260) is the second worst in the Cardinals' franchise history. It marked the end of a four-year stretch that accounts for the four worst seasons in Cardinals (est. 1882) history. From 1895 to 1898, St. Louis compiled an atrocious 147-395 (.271) record. How bad is that stretch? The Baltimore Orioles were historically terrible in 2018, yet they still won 29% of their games; these Browns only won 27% of their games over a four-year span!

The Spanish-American War ate up the newspaper headlines in 1898, but baseball continued on. This year gave us the first woman to play organized baseball when Lizzie Arlington tossed an inning for Reading of the Eastern League. Also, official scorers were directed for the first time to allow hard hit baseballs that were mishandled by a fielder to be scored as a hit rather than an error. The Boston Beaneaters tied a franchise record with 102 wins; it would be another 95 years until the 1993 Atlanta Braves would break that franchise record. Frank Selee, elected to the Hall of Fame as a manager in 1999, won his fifth and final pennant, all five of them with the Beaneaters.

1899

In 1899, Brooklyn changed its team name from the Bridegrooms to the Superbas and St. Louis ditched the Browns moniker in favor of being called the Perfectos. The Superbas went on to win a franchise-best 101 games and take the NL pennant, finishing 8 games ahead of the Boston Beaneaters, the winners of the past three pennants. The Superbas were aided by some shady dealings when the Baltimore Orioles, a joint-ownership of the two teams, allowed some of the best players from the Orioles to be moved to Brooklyn.

Earle Combs, Waite Hoyt, Judy Johnson, and Jocko Conlan, all members of Cooperstown, were all born in 1899. Combs would go on to be a key player for the Yankees in three of their World Series years; he led the league in triples three times from 1927 to 1930. Hoyt also pitched for the Yankees during three of their titles, recording a 1.83 ERA in 11 career postseason starts. Johnson played 17 seasons in his Negro League career, while Conlan would get inducted into the Hall of Fame as an umpire.

Jack Chesbro, Joe McGinnity, Noodles Hahn, and Deacon Phillippe all threw their first Major League pitch, while Sam Crawford also made his debut. In his rookie season, Crawford would record the first 7 triples of his career on his way to setting the current all-time record of 309 triples. Chesbro would go 6-9 in his debut year with Pittsburgh, on his way to 198 victories in his career. McGinnity had a great start to his career, leading baseball with 28 wins in each of his first two seasons. He'd lead the NL five times in his ten-year career. Hahn led baseball in strikeouts in each of his first three seasons, but would retire due to a dead arm after age 27. Phillippe was worth 4.3 WAR on the mound in '99, and would total 29.5 more in his next dozen seasons.

After playing a Hall of Fame career, Bid McPhee played in his eighteenth and final season. He would return to the big leagues a couple years later in 1901, but this time as a manager. His return would be short-lived, as he would resign from the position after just a season and a half. Jackie Stivetts would also retire in 1899; his .298 career batting average is tops among all players with at least 500 career plate appearances and over half their appearances coming as a pitcher.

Interesting numbers from the 1899 season:
- John McGraw's .547 on-base percentage became a new MLB record, topping Billy Hamilton's .521 from 1894. McGraw's record would stand until 1941, when Ted Williams would break it with his .553 OBP. McGraw would eventually be inducted into the Hall of Fame as a manager, not a player, in what is a huge injustice to his playing career. He led baseball in OBP three times, and his .466 career on-base percentage is third best all time, behind only Ted Williams (.482) and Babe Ruth (.474). Luckily, McGraw has a plaque in Cooperstown regardless.
- McGraw scored 140 runs in 1899, but only drove in 33 due

to his high walk rate, speed on the bases, and batting order position. McGraw is the second most recent player to score 100 more runs than he drove in; Lloyd Waner scored 133 and drove in only 27 in 1927.

- Buck Freeman hit 25 triples for the Washington Senators in 1899, which would be a rookie record today if it wasn't for Jimmy Williams. As the starting third baseman for the Pittsburgh Pirates, Williams cracked 27 triples in 1899 to steal the rookie record from Freeman before he ever had a chance to own it.

- Freeman's 25 home runs were also tied for the second most in the 19th Century, behind only Ned Williamson and tied with Fred Pfeffer's 1884 seasons with the Chicago White Stockings.

- Willie Keeler, Brooklyn's star right fielder, finished the season with 633 PA and just two strikeouts. This is the first and only known season in which a player has had at least 400 plate appearances in a season and no more than two strikeouts. A completely unfair comparison: in 2016, Chris Davis had 70 games in which he struck out at least twice.

- By the end of the 1899 season, Kid Nichols had accumulated 96.9 WAR for his career. He surpassed Cap Anson's 94.3 WAR to become the new all-time leader in career WAR, a title that Nichols would hold onto for a short 3 years.

- The Cleveland Spiders were outscored 960 to 377 on the road, a run differential of -583. These numbers don't come without a story though. The Spiders' owners, Frank and Stanley Robison, purchased the St. Louis Browns in an auction. The Robisons promptly traded the best players from the Spiders to the now St. Louis Perfectos in return for their worst players. The Cleveland squad was already having trouble drawing crowds in previous seasons and now with their worst team ever, they saw attendance dip under 200 fans per home game. Once July started, Cleveland decided to play as many road games as possible in order to receive more money in ticket sales. The Spiders would finish their final major league season with a 20-134 record, 11-101 on the road. And that's the short story on how you rack up a run differential of -583 on the road.

- Overall, the Spiders finished the season with a run differential of -723. Here's a fun hypothetical: if the Spiders managed to continue playing games in the 1899 season, and instead of being horrible, had the dominance of the 1927 Yankees (outscoring opponents by 2.39 runs per game), it'd take 303 games at that elite level for them to have a positive run differential on the season.

- Most runs allowed by a team in a season:

```
1,252 - Cleveland Spiders (1899)
1,235 - Pittsburgh Alleghenys (1890)
1,199 - Buffalo Bison (1890)
1,199 - Philadelphia Phillies (1930)
1,122 - Washington Senators (1894)
```

- The five pitchers on Cleveland who made more than ten starts on the season combined for a record of 12-98.

- Oftentimes, it's asked whether you'd prefer to be the best player on the worst team, or the worst player on the best team. Well, the Spiders' best player was probably Chief Zimmer, and he only played 20 games. The catcher batted .342/.407/.479 in 81 plate appearances, and was one of two players on the team with even 0.5 WAR on the year. Only one pitcher, Harry Lochhead (0.1 WAR in 3.2 IP) had a positive WAR. The team totaled -16.6 pitching WAR and -4.1 position player WAR.

The 1899 season made for a fitting end to the 1800s. The play in the National League had been evolving at a rapid rate; the hitters were getting stronger, the pitchers were inventing new pitches, and good fielders were becoming more and more common and this season represented all of that. Despite corruption at the ownership level, baseball had never been stronger. Attendances were up. Newspapers were filling more space with box scores and stories. Baseball had already become America's game.

1900

1900 saw a sizable reduction in the amount of teams in the league and season length. Cutting the size from twelve teams to eight, the National League saw the following teams remaining, in order of their 1900 win total: Brooklyn Superbas, Pittsburgh Pirates, Philadelphia Phillies, Boston Beaneaters, St. Louis Cardinals, Chicago Orphans, Cincinnati Reds, and New York Giants. To go along with the drop in the number of teams, the National League saw a decrease in games on the schedule as they returned to a 140-game schedule. The *Pittsburgh Chronicle Telegraph* offered a silver trophy to the winner of a best of five series between the top two teams, leading to a Brooklyn 3-1 series victory over the Pirates in the first and only *Chronicle-Telegraph* Cup.

Six Hall of Fame players were born in 1900: Lefty Grove, Ted Lyons, Goose Goslin, Gabby Hartnett, Hack Wilson, and Jim Bottomley. Grove won an all-time best nine ERA titles, and would win 300 games on the dot. Lyons would play 21 seasons for the White Sox, and also serve in World War II. Goslin won a batting title in 1928, and would finish with exactly 500 career doubles. Hartnett was the Cubs catcher for most of his career, including his 1935 MVP season. His teammate, center fielder Hack Wilson, would set a still-standing RBI record with 191 in 1930. Bottomley played for their rival Cardinals; he'd rack up a historic 42 double,

20 triple, 31 home run season in 1928.

19-year-old Christy Mathewson debuted in 1900, going 0-3 with a 5.08 ERA in 33.2 IP. It'd be the only time in his career that his ERA was worse than 3.60.

Interesting numbers from the 1900 season:

- John McGraw became the first player with back-to-back seasons of a .500 on-base percentage. Only Babe Ruth and Barry Bonds have since joined him on that list. Over the last three seasons, McGraw had drawn 321 walks while only striking out 43 times, all while maintaining a .507 on-base percentage.
- Honus Wagner led the league in OPS (1.007) for the first of eight times in his career. However, he would never top the 1.000 mark again in his career. Wagner was the only player in baseball that year to reach 300 total bases.
- Wagner became the first player in Pirates history with 200 hits and 70 extra base hits in a season. No Pittsburgh player would do it again until Kiki Cuyler in 1925. Honus led baseball with 45 doubles, 22 triples, and 302 total bases.
- Willie Keeler racked up his seventh season of 200 hits. Only nine other players in MLB history have that many such seasons to their name.
- Beaneaters shortstop Herman Long led the league with a dozen home runs. He slashed a not-too-great .261/.325/.391, especially considering the homer title.
- Roy Thomas put together his second consecutive season with 115 walks and 130 runs. The only other players with multiple such seasons in a row? Cupid Childs, Babe Ruth, Lou Gehrig, and Ted Williams. It would be the first of five consecutive

seasons that Thomas would lead the sport in walks.

- Thomas, who was only playing in his second season at the time, became the only player in MLB history with 100 walks in both of his first two seasons. He'd end up doing it in each of his first six.
- Rube Waddell finished second in the NL in strikeouts (130) despite placing 31st in batters faced (838). His 5.6 K/9 was by far the most in the NL that year (second best was 3.9).
- Joe McGinnity led baseball in wins for the second time in his career... and it was only his second season. The 29-year-old now had 28 wins in each of his first two big league seasons. He'd go on to lead his league in wins thrice more in his career, winning an ERA title in five of his ten seasons.
- Like with wins, the MLB strikeout title was also won by a sophomore who had earned it in his rookie year. "Noodles" Hahn, a starter for the Reds, whiffed a league-best 132 opposing batters after leading the league with 145 as a rookie the year before.
- At age 30, Kid Nichols became the youngest pitcher to reach the 300 career win mark. To this date, no player younger than Nichols has achieved this feat.

The National League had now been around for a quarter century. It had survived three other leagues that have tried to steal its crown (American Association, Union Association, and Players League), but failed to do so. They've been alone at the top for the past nine years, but that was all about to permanently change in 1901 with the creation of the American League.

1901

Welcome to the American League Era! With the official formation of the American League (AL), the sport finally became structured in the way it remains today. The AL originally featured eight teams: the Chicago White Stockings (White Sox), Boston Americans, Detroit Tigers, Philadelphia Athletics, Baltimore Orioles, Washington Senators, Cleveland Bluebirds (Blues), and Milwaukee Brewers. The eight National League teams remained the same from 1900. Several popular players made the move from the NL to the AL. The American League's Chicago White Sox (83-53) and National League's Pittsburgh Pirates (90-49) won their respective league's pennant, but there would be no World Series played between the AL and NL until 1903.

Hall of Fame outfielder Heinie Manush was born in 1901. He'd average 204 hits, 62 extra base hits, and 104 runs per 162 games in his 17 seasons in the big leagues.

Most notably, Eddie Plank, Doc White, Terry Turner, and Earl Moore made their debuts in 1901. Plank completed 28 games in 1901; he'd complete at least 20 in each of his first dozen seasons. White went 14-13 in his rookie year, finishing with a 3.19 ERA. He would improve on his ERA in each of the next five seasons. Turner went 3-for-7 in his two game stint with the Pirates, but wouldn't return until 1904 with Cleveland, where he would spend most of his career. Moore racked up 4.9 WAR as a rookie, the most he'd put up in a season in his 20s.

Billy Hamilton, who currently ranks third all time in stolen bases, and Amos Rusie, who won five strikeout titles and a Pitching Triple Crown, both played their final games in 1901. Hamilton would be posthumously elected into the Hall of Fame in 1961 by the Veterans Committee and Rusie would join him in 1977 via that same committee.

Interesting numbers from the 1901 season:
- Athletics player Nap Lajoie hit a staggering .426, an American League record that has not since been broken. Some see Lajoie's .426 as the highest batting average of all time; however, that mark belongs to Hugh Duffy's 1894 season in which he hit .440.
- Lajoie also became the second player in MLB history (Duffy's record setting 1894 season being the first) with 150 singles and 75 extra base hits in a season. That club now currently features twelve individual seasons, only one of which has come since World War II (Don Mattingly in 1986). Lajoie is one of two middle infielders on this list, being joined by second baseman Rogers Hornsby 20 seasons later.
- Amazingly, despite what remains the best average in AL history, Lajoie's .463 on-base percentage ranks a measly 60th among all American League qualifiers. Mike Trout's 2018 on-base percentage was .460, despite a batting average over 100 points lower than Lajoie. Causing his extremely low OBP for such a high batting average was his almost complete lack of walks. Only Kirby Puckett (23 walks in 1988) has had fewer

walks in a 225 hit season than Lajoie's 24.

- Nap's 1.106 OPS is the highest in MLB history by a player with a strikeout percentage of 2% or lower.
- Only three players in the 20th century or later have led their league in home runs in the same year that they batted .400. They are: Nap Lajoie (1901), Rogers Hornsby (1922 and 1925), and Ted Williams (1941).
- Willie Keeler had his eighth and final 200-hit season. He is responsible for all eight of the 200 hit seasons by players 5'5" or shorter (he was 5'4").
- Keeler is one of only two players in MLB history with eight consecutive 200-hit seasons (also Ichiro, with ten).
- John McGraw only played in 73 games, but once again reached base more often than not (.508 on-base percentage). It was the third time in a row that he had a .500 OBP, and he maintained a .350/.500/.418 slash line from 1897-1901.
- On July 10, Philadelphia Athletics' first baseman Harry Davis collected the first cycle in American League history. In his 22-year career, Davis led the Majors in doubles twice, triples once, and homers twice. Seems that he was a fitting player for the first cycle.
- Brooklyn's Jimmy Sheckard hit grand slams in back-to-back games on September 23 and 24. He finished his career with only three grand slams.
- Americans starting pitcher Cy Young had a historic season on the mound, going 33-10 with a 1.62 ERA and 158 strikeouts, good enough for the Pitching Triple Crown in the AL. Young's 219 ERA+ is tied for the eighth best mark in a qualified season by an AL pitcher with Blake Snell's historic 2018 season. The next highest ERA+ in 1901 was 154, by Beaneaters pitcher Vic Willis.

- Young also led the Majors in walks per nine innings (as in, he averaged the fewest) for the ninth consecutive season. In that span, dating back to 1893, Young walked 553 batters in 3,390.2 innings, good for a rate of only 1.5 walks per 9.
- Noodles Hahn led the Majors in strikeouts for the third time in as many seasons. The Reds ace had a 2.87 ERA and 516 strikeouts through his first three big league seasons.
- National League pitchers Noodles Hahn, Bill Donovan, Tom Hughes, and Christy Mathewson all recorded 220+ strikeouts in 1901. It would take another 62 years before four NL pitchers reached the 220 strikeout mark in the same season again.
- Since 1893, when the mound was moved back to its current distance, the 1901 season marked the only year in which two rookies (Tom Hughes and Christy Mathewson) tossed 220 strikeouts in the same season.

Highlighted by the dominance of Triple Crown winners Nap Lajoie and Cy Young, the American League's debut season featured several statistical extremes. Additionally, the founding of the AL saw the beginning of several franchises that still exist today, including the White Sox, Red Sox, Tigers, Athletics, Orioles (who were actually the Brewers in 1901, not the Orioles), Indians (Blues/Bluebirds), and Twins (formerly the Senators). The Baltimore Orioles were the only AL team from 1901 to not make it to the present day, they would phase out after just two seasons.

1902

Besides the Cleveland Bluebirds unofficially becoming the "Bronchos" and the Milwaukee Brewers becoming the St. Louis Browns, the league as a whole remained the same entering the 1902 season. Similar to the AL's debut season, there would be no World Series played between the American League and National League pennant winners. The 83-53 Philadelphia Athletics won their first ever AL pennant, while their intrastate Pittsburgh Pirates easily won the National League with a staggering 103-36 record, 27.5 games ahead of the second place Brooklyn Superbas. Pittsburgh managed to win 20 more games than any other team in 1902.

Al Simmons, Earl Averill, and Red Lucas were all born in 1902. Simmons would go on to win multiple batting titles and also win back-to-back World Series with the Athletics. Averill would be selected to six consecutive All Star Games at the peak of his career; his son, Earl, also played in the Majors. Lucas would total 44.2 WAR in his fifteen seasons.

Pud Galvin, MLB's first 300-game winner and thrower of two no hitters, and Fred Dunlap, who led the Union Association in most major batting categories in its one year existence, both died in 1902.

Joe Tinker, Johnny Evers, George Mullin, and Addie Joss all debuted in 1902. Tinker and Evers would become a famous double play combo for the Cubs, while Mullin would play most of his career in Detroit, where he accumulated 35.0 pitching WAR. However, Mullin also was great with the bat for a pitcher, finishing his career with a 100 OPS+ (league average, for any position) in 1,691 PA. Joss would record a 1.114 WHIP as a rookie, but go on to become MLB's all-time leader in the category, finishing his career with a 0.968 mark.

Catcher Wilbert Robinson, who would later be inducted into Baseball's Hall of Fame as a manager, played his final game in 1902. Robinson played in seventeen seasons in the bigs. In addition, Win Mercer pitched in his final season, ending his career on a high note. His 6.0 WAR is the second most by a pitcher in his final season in the Modern Era, behind only Sandy Koufax's 10.3 in 1966.

via Wikimedia Commons

Interesting numbers from the 1902 season:
- Cleveland's Bill Bradley set an American League record with a home run in four consecutive games. Looking even further Bradley had eight career home runs to his name before his record setting streak; he then added on eight more in a span of just over a month from May 21 to June 30 (including four in his streak).
- On the final day of his home run tear, Bradley and teammates Nap Lajoie and Charlie Hickman became the first American League trio to hit three consecutive home runs.
- Ed Delahanty led the Majors with a 1.043 OPS. Impressively, he totaled 43 doubles, fourteen triples, and ten home runs

to only nine strikeouts (he had 60 strikeouts the year before). It was the third baseman's fourth and final time leading the Majors in OPS, as 1902 would be Delahanty's final full season.

- Roy Thomas' 437 walks through four seasons is the most in National League history. The outfielder also led the NL in on-base percentage for the first time, at .414, despite it being the worst mark of his career.

- Reds outfielder Sam Crawford led the Majors in triples, with 22 on the season. It'd be the first of five seasons he'd lead all of baseball in three-baggers, on his way to a record 309 career triples. Through 1902, Crawford had 60 career triples to 56 doubles.

- Honus Wagner edged out Crawford to lead the National League in slugging percentage. Wagner's .463 SLG may have been tops in the NL, but he'd finish a distant eighth place on the Major League leaderboard, thanks in part to the American League not yet adopting the foul strike rule for its first two seasons. The seven players in the AL with a higher slugging percentages than Wagner slugged .500 or better.

- Teammates Fred Clarke and Honus Wagner would tie for the Major League lead in hit by pitches with fourteen apiece. It would be another 68 years before the next Pirates hitter would get hit that many times in a season and another 102 years until the next set of Pirates teammates would get plunked by 14 pitches in the same season.

- Over the course of the entire season, the Pittsburgh Pirates never had a losing streak of longer than two games.

- The Chicago White Sox had six players steal 30 or more bases in 1902. Six! The only other American League team to have that many guys pick 30 bases in a season was the run-happy 1976 Oakland Athletics, who own the AL record for most stolen bases in a season with 341.

- The Bronchos as a team set a 20th century record by committing six errors in one inning on June 2.
- Cy Young became MLB's all-time leader in WAR, finishing the year at 116.6. Young surpassed Kid Nichols' mark of 108.3, and wouldn't be topped himself until Babe Ruth came along.
- A 21-year-old Christy Mathewson posted a 14-17 (.452) record for the New York Giants, despite tying for the Major League lead with eight shutouts on the season. With his fourteen wins and eight shutouts, Mathewson became the first pitcher in MLB history to record double digit wins in a season and have more than half of those wins come via the shutout. To this day, he remains the only Giants pitcher to ever have such a season.
- Although the save stat was not official at the time, Vic Willis managed to lead the Majors in both complete games (45) and saves (3). He also struck out an NL-best 225 batters.
- In the AL, 25-year-old Athletics starter Rube Waddell led the league with 210 strikeouts. It'd be the first year of a six season streak in which he led the AL in K in each year.

1902 saw dominance in Pittsburgh and the title of "Greatest of All Time" being unofficially passed on to Cy Young. Cleveland still couldn't figure out what they wanted to be called; they wouldn't settle on the "Indians" for another dozen years.

1903

The New York Highlanders (Yankees) will play their first season in franchise history after replacing the Baltimore Orioles in the American League. The Bronchos nickname for the Cleveland squad would last just one season, as they would return to their original nickname of the Naps in 1903. Also making a name change this year was the National League team located in Chicago; they would drop the Orphans name to become the Cubs that we all know today. The American League finally adopts the foul strike rule (foul balls would be counted as strikes unless the hitter already had two strikes) two years after the National League installed it into their rules book; the foul strike rule is considered one of the biggest factors leading to the Dead Ball Era. The Boston Americans (91-47) would defeat the Pittsburgh Pirates (91-49) five games to three in a best-of-nine World Series in the first ever postseason played that was not considered an exhibition.

Lou Gehrig, Mickey Cochrane, Charlie Gehringer, Carl Hubbell, Paul Waner, Tony Lazzeri, Travis Jackson, Chick Hafey, Cool Papa Bell, Walter O'Malley, and Tom Yawkey were all born in 1903 and would all eventually be inducted into the Hall of Fame. These eleven are the most Hall of Famers ever born in the same calendar year. Gehrig would finish with a 1.080 career OPS and six championship rings. Cochrane won a couple MVPs (as did Gehrig), while his four-year teammate Gehringer won multiple hit titles. Hubbell led baseball in ERA three times in a four-year span, while Waner won a trio of batting titles and led the league in triples in each of his first two seasons. Lazzeri would be the second baseman on several World Series Yankees teams, while Jackson would man shortstop for their fellow New York team, the Giants. In his most dominant five-year stretch, Hafey maintained a 1.009 OPS for the Cardinals. Bell played center field for 25 years in the Negro Leagues. O'Malley was the owner who brought the Dodgers to Los Angeles, while Yawkey would serve as owner of the Red Sox for 44 years.

After falling, or possibly jumping, into the Niagara River, Ed Delahanty was found at the bottom of Horseshoe Falls, dead at 35 years old. Delahanty would be inducted to Cooperstown in 1945. Also passing away in 1903 was William Van Winkle "Chicken" Wolf, the only player to play in all ten seasons that the American Association existed; he was 41 years old.

Mordecai Brown and Chief Bender make their Major League debuts in 1903, pitching for the St. Louis Cardinals and the Philadelphia Athletics respectively. While Bender would stay with the Athletics and play most of his career in Philadelphia, Brown made a name for himself in Chicago for the Cubbies.

George Van Haltren would play the final game of his 17 year career. His eleven seasons of 100+ runs and 175+ hits has only been matched by Ty Cobb, Lou Gehrig, Stan Musial, Hank Aaron, and Derek Jeter, with Jeter being the only one with more than eleven such seasons. Jeter would do it 13 times.

Interesting numbers from the 1903 season:

- Death, taxes, and Roy Thomas getting on base: the outfielder drew 107 walks on his way to an MLB-leading .453 on-base percentage.
- Best OBP through five seasons in the Majors (minimum 2,500 plate appearances):

```
.484 - Ted Williams
.449 - Frank Thomas
.443 - Roy Thomas
.435 - Wade Boggs
```

- Cy Seymour's .382 OBP ranked 15th in the National League. His OBP was higher than every qualified American Leaguer except for Jimmy Barrett (.407 OBP) of the Detroit Tigers.
- Frank Chance swiped 67 bases, the most for a first baseman in a season since 1900. His 378 career stolen bases barely edges out George Sisler's 375 for the most career steals by a player who primarily played the position.
- Fred Clarke (164 OPS+) and Honus Wagner (160 OPS+), became the first Pirates teammates to qualify for the batting title and end the season with OPS+ of at least 160. The only other duo in Pirates franchise history to accomplish this would be Roberto Clemente and Willie Stargell in 1969. They had an OPS+ of 168 and 163, respectively.
- Through 2018, there have been 21 triples hit in World Series Game Sevens, a third of which were hit in the first official World Series. Fred Clarke and Kitty Bransfield each had a triple for the Pittsburgh Pirates while Jimmy Collins, Hobe

Ferris, Buck Freeman, Freddy Parent, and Chick Stahl were responsible for the five triples hit by the Boston Americans.

- Henry Schmidt, a 30-year-old rookie of the Brooklyn Superbas, tossed 301 innings on his way to a 22-13 record. Schmidt would elect to not sign a contract in 1904, citing his unwillingness to live on the east coast. He remains the only pitcher in history to win twenty games in his sole major league season.

- Rube Waddell's 302 strikeouts for the Philadelphia Athletics was 125 more than the next closest American League pitcher, Bill Donovan, who finished the season with 187 strikeouts. The only other pitcher to ever lead the American League by that many strikeouts in a season was California Angels' Nolan Ryan. He finished the 1973 season exactly 125 strikeouts ahead of Bert Blyleven.

- In his second season in the Majors, Addie Joss led baseball with a 0.948 WHIP. It'd be one of two times that Joss led all pitchers in that category, and his 0.968 career mark is the best in the sport's history.

The 1903 season would be the second to last time that MLB played a 140 game schedule. The league's schedule went up to 154 games for the next 15 seasons until bringing back the 140 game schedule for one more season in 1919. As it goes for us stat hunters, it is pretty convenient that the 140 game schedule would die with the Dead Ball Era.

1904

1904 ended baseball's one year streak of holding a World Series for the pennant winner of each league. John T. Brush, owner of the NL champion New York Giants (106-47), declined to play the AL champion Boston Americans (95-59). On the opposite end of the spectrum, the Washington Senators finished with an abysmal 38-113 record (.252 winning percentage), good (or bad) for the second worst W-L% by an American League team.

Buddy Myer and Chuck Klein were both born in 1904. Myer would average only thirteen stolen bases per 162 games in his career, but he would lead the league with 30 in 1928. Klein, who played many of his home games at the hitter-friendly Baker Bowl, put up incredible home batting numbers over the course of his career. He finished his career with a 1.027 home OPS and .813 road OPS.

Fred Carroll, owner of the second best single-season OBP in Pittsburgh franchise history (.486 in 1889) died in 1904.

Ed Walsh and Sherry Magee both made their debuts in 1904. Walsh would win multiple ERA titles in his 14 season career, and Magee would win multiple RBI crowns.

Dan Brouthers and Jim O'Rourke played their *final* games in 1904. At the time of their retirements, they both ranked in the top ten in the career hits list with nearly 5,000 combined in their careers. O'Rourke had already called it quits following the 1893 season, but the 53-year-old returned for a last game, going 1-for-4 for the Giants. By doing so, he became the oldest player in National League history to record a hit.

Interesting numbers from the 1904 season:
- Roy Thomas drew 102 walks, leading all of MLB for the fifth consecutive season. He is the only player in MLB history to lead the sport in walks five years in a row. The only other player to lead his respective league in walks drawn in five consecutive years is Barry Bonds, who led the National League each year from 2000-2004, exactly 100 years after Thomas' streak.
- John Anderson, one of three Norwegian-born players in Major League Baseball history, capped off an extremely consistent three year stretch in 1904. His three seasons leading up to, and including 1904:

> 1902: .284/.316/.385
> 1903: .284/.312/.385
> 1904: .278/.313/.385

- While splitting time playing for the Boston Americans and the New York Highlanders, Patsy Dougherty ended up scoring 113 runs to lead all of baseball in that category. In fact, Dougherty wound up being the only player to reach the century mark in runs scored in 1904. Only one other season in the Modern Era has had just one player score 100+ runs, the 1919 season. That one player? None other than Babe Ruth.

- Cardinals catcher Mike Grady had a historic offensive season given his position, slashing .313/.376/.474. His 167 OPS+ would not be topped by another catcher with 100 games played until Mike Piazza's 1995 season, where he posted a 172 OPS+.

- Hobe Ferris, second baseman for the Boston Americans, didn't have the season you'd hope to get out of a player with 602 plate appearances. Ferris finished the year with a paltry 120 base hits, 23 walks, and one hit by pitch. Of the 6,852 player-seasons with 600+ plate appearances from 1876 to 2018, his .245 OBP is the lowest of them all.

- The Detroit Tigers played their way to ten ties during the 1904 season and would make up eight of those games. Their 162 games played in 1904 would remain a record until the American League expanded their schedule to 162 games in 1961. Detroit's Jimmy Barrett played center field every game that year, making him the only player to play 162 games in a season for the first 85 years of baseball.

- On May 5, Cy Young tossed a perfect game against the Philadelphia Athletics. This was the third perfect game in MLB history, and the first of the Modern Era. To this day, he is the only pitcher in Boston Red Sox franchise history (the Americans would become the Red Sox) to throw a perfect game.

- Over the course of the season, Young struck out 200 batters while only walking 29. He remains the only pitcher in American League history with 200 strikeouts and fewer than

30 walks in a season.

- Young's Americans are the third most recent team to use only five starting pitchers in an entire season; it's since been done by the 1966 Dodgers and 2003 Mariners. Along with Young, Boston also started Bill Dinneen, Norwood Gibson, Jesse Tannehill, and George Winter. Winter's 2.32 ERA was the *worst* of the five.

- For the second consecutive season, Athletics ace Rube Waddell posted a K/9 of over 8.0. They were the first two such seasons in American League history. The next pitcher to average eight strikeouts per nine innings in consecutive qualified seasons would be Herb Score in 1955 and 1956. Waddell's 349 strikeouts were the most in baseball by over 100.

- Ned Garvin's 1.72 ERA is the best among pitchers to win less than 30% of their decisions. Garvin pitched for both the Superbas and Highlanders, and went 5-16 despite an ERA+ of 160.

- Jack Chesbro recorded 239 strikeouts for the New York Highlanders, finishing second behind Rube Waddell for the American League lead. His teammate, Jack Powell would wind up third on the AL leaderboard with 202 punchouts. This would be the only year in either of these pitchers' careers in which they would reach the 200-strikeout mark, but nonetheless their 1904 season would go down in Yankees franchise history. It would take 97 more years before another Yankee duo, Roger Clemens and Mike Mussina, would strike out 200+ in the same season. To this day, Chesbro and Powell, along with Clemens and Moose, are the only pitching pairs in Yankee history to each punch out 200 opposing batters in a season.

- Joe McGinnity, appropriately nicknamed Iron Man, tossed 408 innings worth of work to lead the National League. It's the 123rd and final time a National League pitcher would eclipse the 400 innings pitched mark in a season. McGinnity threw 434 innings the previous year, giving him the honor of throwing the last two 400-frame seasons in the NL.
- 1904 was the first year in MLB history that saw ten qualified pitchers with an ERA below 2.00.
- The worst ERA by a pitcher in 1904 was 4.25 by Tom Fisher. A 4.25 ERA would be considered near average in today's game.
- The league average run per game mark of 3.73 per team per game marked a new MLB low. It'd been the first season ever in which offenses failed to score an average of four runs per game. Just a decade before in 1894, teams were scoring an average of 7.38 runs per game.

As highlighted by some incredible pitching numbers, 1904 marked what is considered the beginning of an offensive drought that would last until Babe Ruth entered the league and popularized the home run ball at the beginning of the 1920s, coinciding with the beginning of the "Live Ball Era" and the next book in our series.

1905

And… the World Series returns! The 105-48 New York Giants topped the Philadelphia Athletics four games to one in baseball's second World Series. The Series featured only shutouts. Philadelphia barely won the AL pennant, finishing four games ahead in the loss column, but none in the win column, over the Chicago White Sox. Off the field, the mother of soon to be Major Leaguer Ty Cobb shot and killed her husband, Ty's father, mistaking him for a burglar. Cobb said that he set out to honor his father's legacy with his playing style, who never got to see him play.

Wally Berger, Bob Johnson, Rick Ferrell, Freddie Lindstrom, Red Ruffing, and Leo Durocher were all born in 1905. Berger, a center fielder, would lead the NL with 34 homers and 130 RBI in 1935. Bob Johnson (one of four men named Bob Johnson to play in MLB history) led the AL in OBP in 1944. Lindstrom would play 1,807 games in the field in his career, all coming at catcher. Ruffing would win six World Series with the Yankees, going 7-2 in the postseason himself. Durocher, a shortstop in his time as a player, would go on to manage the Dodgers, Cubs, Giants, and Astros in his 24 year Hall-worthy managerial career.

Pete Browning, one of seventeen qualified players in MLB history to sport a .340 lifetime batting average, died at the age of 44. He had a staggering 223 OPS+ as a rookie in 1882.

Ty Cobb and Eddie Cicotte both made their debuts for Detroit during the 1905 season. Cicotte would pitch in three games for the Tigers in 1905, but wouldn't return to the Majors until 1908 with Boston. Cobb, on the other hand, would play his first 22 seasons in Detroit. He'd end up totaling over 4,000 hits with an MLB-best .366 career batting average.

Jesse Burkett played his final campaign in 1905. Over the course of his career, he led the National League in batting average three times, including back-to-back seasons with a .400 mark.

Interesting numbers from the 1905 season:
- Cy Seymour totaled 40 doubles, 21 triples, and 121 RBI in 1905. He is one of five players in MLB history to reach all three of those marks in a single season. Before him, the last player to do it was Nap Lajoie in 1897. The Reds outfielder led the Majors in both hits and total bases. His .377 batting average in 1905 still sits atop the Cincinnati Reds' record book, a record book that has 137 years worth of history.
- Honus Wagner put up what was, at the time, the best season ever seen by a position player in MLB history, becoming the first position player ever with ten wins above replacement in a single season. Amazingly, he didn't lead the National League in any other major batting category, but his 50 extra base hits and 50 stolen bases paired with elite defense from the shortstop position amounted to a staggering WAR figure.
- A lot of great hitters have played in the outfield for the Giants franchise; Mays, Bonds, Ott, Youngs, Cepeda, and Bonds to name a few, but none of those guys have more hits in a season

than Mike Donlin. His 216 hits in 1905 ranks seventh in Giants franchise history, but still sits atop all the outfielders that have played for the Giants during their first 136 years of existence.

- While Roy Thomas' walk title streak ended at five seasons, he still led the Majors by reaching base 275 times.
- The player who ended Roy Thomas' walk title streak was Topsy Hartsel, who totaled 121 free passes for the Philadelphia A's in 1905. Hartsel's 121 walks is the most by an American Leaguer who finished the season without a home run. Only Eddie Stanky's 1946 season with the Brooklyn Dodgers saw a player rack up more base on balls without a homer.
- Future Hall of Famer Elmer Flick led the American League with a .308 batting average. It would remain the lowest batting average to win a batting title for 63 years, when Carl Yastrzemski's .301 batting average in 1968 would surpass it. As of the writing of this book, Flick's .308 BA is still the second lowest to ever take home a batting title.
- New York Giants ace Christy Mathewson won the National League's Pitching Triple Crown, going 31-9 with a 1.28 ERA and 206 strikeouts. He became the first of what would be two pitchers (Walter Johnson in 1913) to win 30 games in a season with less than 10 losses and a sub-1.30 ERA.
- Christy Mathewson also became the only pitcher in MLB history to pitch a shutout in three games in the same World Series. Additionally, he's the only pitcher to toss three total shutouts in the same postseason. Going along with one more World Series shutout in 1913, Mathewson is the only pitcher in MLB history with four career World Series shutouts.
- Rube Waddell struck out 250 batters for the third consecutive

season. He now owned three of the four 250 strikeout seasons in the Modern Era, the other belonging to Christy Mathewson in 1903. It was the third of what would be five consecutive years that Waddell led the Majors in strikeouts. His 1.48 ERA in 1905 was a career low. Waddell also won the Pitching Triple Crown, but for the American League.

- Here's his name again: Cy Young became the first qualified pitcher in the Modern Era (three 1880s guys did it) with a K/BB ratio of 7 or better and a sub-2.00 ERA in a season. It would be 90 years before anyone did it again. Since Young's 1905 season, only Greg Maddux, Pedro Martinez, and Clayton Kershaw have added their names to that list. Young also became the first (and only player so far) to lead the Red Sox in WAR in five consecutive seasons. Mookie Betts could become the second in 2019.

- Detroit's Ed Killian became the only pitcher in MLB history to face 1,200 batters in consecutive years and not allow a home run. He faced 2,601 batters from 1904-1905 and didn't surrender a single homer.

- The Chicago Cubs became the first team in MLB history to have *six* qualified pitchers with an ERA below 3.00. Ed Reulbach led the way at 1.42. The '05 Cubs would only be joined by the 1916 Brooklyn Robins as teams to accomplish this feat.

- Those six Cubs pitchers with an ERA under 3.00 were Buttons Briggs, Mordecai Brown, Carl Lundgren, Ed Reulbach, Jake Weimer, and Bob Wicker. They make up the only group of six teammates that all qualified for the ERA title and posted an ERA+ greater than 130 in the same season.

With their 105 wins on the season, the New York Giants became the first team in MLB history with back-to-back 100-win seasons. Meanwhile, on the other side of town, the Brooklyn Superbas would lose a franchise record 104 games; the 104 losses remains the worst season in Dodgers franchise history. Aces Rube Waddell and Christy Mathewson continued their historic dominance on the mound, becoming the first pair of pitchers in MLB history to win Triple Crowns in the same season. It would only happen three more times.

1906

1906 was best known for its cross-city World Series and the Chicago Cubs' historic (regular) season. Besides falling four games to two in the World Series to the 93-58 White Sox, the Cubs' season was all positives, finishing the year with an incredible 116-36 record. Although many think of the 2001 Mariners as the winningest team in baseball history, their 116-46 record is actually five games worse in the standings than the 1906 Cubs' 116-36 campaign. In the end, neither team won the World Series in their 116-win campaigns. The White Sox won the World Series in spite of a .198 series batting average and 15 errors in six games.

Joe Cronin, Tommy Bridges, and Lloyd Waner were born in 1906. Cronin would finish his career with 2,285 base hits. Of the 37 shortstops to reach the 2,000 hit mark, Cronin's lifetime .468 SLG ranks number one. Bridges won a pair of American League strikeout titles while pitching solely for the Detroit Tigers throughout his sixteen years in the big leagues; his sixteen seasons with the club is the most by a pitcher in Tigers franchise history. Waner would record more than 220 hits in each of his first three seasons in the Majors and his 678 hits from 1927 to 1929 is the most by any player in their first three seasons.

Hall of Famer Buck Ewing died at the age of 47. Ewing's 53

stolen bases in 1888 are the second-most by a catcher in MLB history. He's also the only catcher to record 10+ triples in three consecutive seasons, and he did it twice - the first time from 1883 to 1885 and the second time from 1888 to 1890.

Eddie Collins and Babe Adams debuted in 1906. Collins would go on to win the AL Chalmers Award in 1914, and he currently ranks eleventh on the all-time hits leaderboard with his 3,315 career base hits. Adams would pitch 18 seasons with the Pittsburgh Pirates, winning a championship in his second season with the team and his second-to-last season with the team.

Kid Nichols, Hugh Duffy, and Sam Thompson all played their final career games in 1906. Nichols, MLB's youngest 300 game winner, retired with 362 career wins and a 2.96 ERA. Hugh Duffy's .440 batting average in 1894 is a record that will likely never be broken. Thompson, known for his incredible knack for driving in runs, finished with 1,308 RBI in 1,410 games, including a record 61 in one month in August 1894. The 46-year-old hadn't played in the Majors since 1898, but then returned in '06, going 7-for-31 as a member of the Tigers.

Interesting numbers from the 1906 season:
- Left fielder George Stone totaled 208 base hits for the St. Louis Browns in 1906. He didn't lead the American League in hits that season, but he did lead the league in batting average, on-base percentage, and slugging percentage. Oddly enough, Stone did lead the AL in strikeouts. Out of the 534 player seasons in which a hitter recorded 200+ hits, he and Babe Ruth (1924) are the only players to lead their league in all three of the slash categories and strikeouts in the same season.

- 1906 is the only year in Major League Baseball's history that three teams in the same league won at least 40 of their first 60 games (Cubs, Giants, and Pirates). In fact, only six other times have even two teams in the same league won 40 out of their first 60, with the most recent being the Red Sox and Yankees in 2018, and the next most recent being the Dodgers and Giants in 1962.
- Cleveland shortstop Terry Turner's 5.4 defensive WAR from 1906 is the second best in a single season in MLB history, behind only Andrelton Simmons' 5.5 from 2013.
- The Cleveland Naps' middle infield, led by Nap Lajoie and the aforementioned Turner, is the only middle infield in MLB history to have two players with seven or more WAR. Both blew away that minimum with 10.0 from Lajoie and 9.4 from Turner. The duo finished first and second in WAR in the Majors, edging out Pittsburgh shortstop Honus Wagner's 9.3.
- Additionally, Lajoie and Turner became the first position player duo to each put up 9 WAR in a season. They would later be joined by only the 1927, 1928, and 1930 Yankees (Babe Ruth and Lou Gehrig), and the 1996 Mariners (Ken Griffey Jr., Álex Rodríguez).
- Brooklyn outfielder Billy Maloney struck out 116 times and failed to hit a home run. He is the only player in MLB history to strike out 110 times in a season with zero home runs. Additionally, his 116 strikeouts were, at the time, an MLB single-season high, topping Sam Wise's mark of 104 set in 1884.
- Spike Shannon led the National League in games played in 1906 while splitting his time between playing for the St. Louis Cardinals and the New York Giants. He'd finish the season with 151 base hits, tied for 22nd in MLB that year, and just

ten extra base hits. His 162 total bases and .275 slugging percentage are the lowest in a season in MLB history by a player with at least a 150 hits.

- For the fourth time in his career, Roy Thomas racked up 100 walks in a season without hitting a home run. He is responsible for a quarter of the sixteen seasons in which a player didn't hit a homer and still totaled 100+ walks. Max Bishop accomplished this feat in 1926 and 1927, making him the only one besides Thomas to have multiple such seasons.

- Mordecai "Three Finger" Brown's 1.04 ERA in 1906 is the third best by a qualified pitcher in MLB history, and the lowest by a pitcher with 20 wins. Nine of his 32 starts would end in shutouts. Needless to say, his 1.04 ERA is a Cubs franchise record, but unfortunately for his Cubs, he allowed seven earned runs in 1.2 innings pitched in the sixth and final game of the World Series.

- Fellow Cubs starter Ed Reulbach set an MLB record by allowing only 5.3 hits per nine innings pitched (he allowed 129 hits in 218.0 innings). Such a feat (allowing hits at a lower clip in a season than Reulbach did in 1906) has only occurred four times since (Nolan Ryan twice, Luis Tiant, and Pedro Martinez).

- The Cubs became the first of what would be three Modern Era teams to post a 1.75 ERA or better. They would be joined by their 1907 and 1909 teams.

- In 1906, Ed Walsh tossed ten shutouts to become the first White Sox pitcher to reach the double digit mark in shutouts. Two years later, Walsh would break his own franchise record by recording eleven shutouts. He is one of just two pitchers to have multiple seasons with ten shutouts, Grover Cleveland Alexander being the other. Walsh is the only White Sox pitcher to ever reach the ten-shutout mark for a season.

- Barney Pelty's 1.59 ERA and Jack Powell's 1.77 ERA for the St. Louis Browns are the two lowest ERA's posted by a qualified pitcher in Browns/Orioles history. Pelty finished the season with a 163 ERA+. The only Orioles pitchers to eclipse that ERA+ in a season all have plaques in the Baseball Hall of Fame (Hoyt Wilhelm, Jim Palmer, and Mike Mussina).
- For the second consecutive season the Boston Beaneaters had four pitchers finish the season with at least twenty losses. To this day, those two Beaneaters teams are the only ones to employ four twenty-game losers.
- Of the 73 pitchers that qualified for the ERA title, 61 had an ERA below 3.00. Not one of those 61 was Cy Young, who still managed to lead baseball with a 1.87 fielding independent pitching (FIP) thanks to 140 strikeouts, 25 walks, and three home runs allowed. His 21 losses led the American League. Talk about unlucky!

Despite being in the midst of baseball's worst offensive droughts in history, Nap Lajoie and Terry Turner put together possibly the best season by a position player duo not named Ruth and Gehrig. However, it was Mordecai Brown and his 116-win Cubs, and their unlikely World Series collapse, that captured the headlines from the 1906 season.

1907

After 24 seasons as the Beaneaters, Boston's baseball team became known as the "Doves." They finished in seventh place in the National League, 47 games behind the 107-45 Chicago Cubs. The Cubs won their first ever World Series, four games to zero (and one tie) over the 92-58 AL Champion Detroit Tigers.

Hall of Famers Jimmie Foxx, Luke Appling, and Bill Dickey were born in 1906. Foxx led baseball in OPS five times in the 1930s, winning himself three MVPs. Appling played all of his 2,422 games for the White Sox and is the franchise's all-time hit leader with 2,749. Dickey caught for the Yankees during the 1930s and 1940s, winning seven rings and making eleven All Star Games.

Charlie Buffinton, who went 48-16 as a 23-year-old pitcher for the Boston Beaneaters in 1884, died at the age of 46. Buffinton's 1884 season remains the only season in which a pitcher struck out 400+ hitters and racked up 90+ hits at the plate. His 417 strikeouts that season is the sixth-highest for a single season and the most in a season for a franchise that still exists today. He finished his 11 year career with 233 wins and currently sits 65th on the all-time wins list.

Baseball legends Walter Johnson and Tris Speaker made their

debuts as nineteen-year-olds. Johnson went 5-9 with a 1.88 ERA and two shutouts in 1907. Johnson would record at least one shutout in each of his 21 big league seasons, all with the Washington Senators, on his way to setting the all-time record of 110 career shutouts. Speaker, on the other hand, didn't fare as well as Johnson. He only went three-for-twenty with three singles in his freshman campaign for the Boston Americans. In fourteen years, during the middle of a game against the Tigers, Tris Speaker will be replaced in center field by another player making his debut. That player? Tex Jeanes, Speaker's nephew. The manager that day? Tris Speaker.

Among those to retire following the 1907 season include John McGraw, Jake Beckley, and Lave Cross. McGraw, best known for his record setting .547 on-base percentage in 1899, finished his career with a .334/.466/.410 slash line. Only Ted Williams and Babe Ruth had a higher career on-base percentage than McGraw. Beckley finished with 2,938 hits in his 20 season career, the fifth most of any first baseman in baseball history. Lave Cross, who totaled 2,651 hits in his 21 year career, is the only player to play for the Philadelphia Athletics of the American Association, the Philadelphia Athletics of the Players League, and the Philadelphia Athletics of the American League. To boot, Cross also spent six seasons with the Philadelphia Phillies.

Interesting numbers from the 1907 season:
- Future Hall of Famer Jimmy Collins set a peculiar record in his penultimate season. His 29 doubles are the most of any player with no triples or home runs in a season. He had 116 singles, 29 doubles, 0 triples, and 0 home runs.
- Not including Cap Anson's National Association days (since

we're not counting that as a Major League), Ty Cobb's 167 OPS+ in 1907 is the second best in a qualified season by a player age 20 or younger. Only Mike Trout's 168 in 2012 was better. For Cobb, it was the beginning of a stretch of nine consecutive seasons in which he would lead the American League in batting average and OPS+.

- With his 61 stolen bases and .921 OPS, Honus Wagner became the first player in MLB history to lead baseball in both categories. He would repeat in the following season.
- MLB batting average race in 1907:

```
.35041 - Ty Cobb (212-for-605)
.34951 - Honus Wagner (180-for-515)
Both averages round to .350, even though Cobb
beat Wagner by nearly a full point.
```

- Athletics ace Rube Waddell led baseball in strikeouts for the fifth consecutive season. Despite an identical 232 strikeouts in 1908, he failed to lead the Majors for a sixth straight. The only other pitcher in the game's history to lead MLB in strikeouts in five consecutive seasons was Randy Johnson from 1998 to 2002.
- Cubs duo Carl Lundgren (18-7, 213 ERA+) and Jack Pfiester (14-9, 216 ERA+) are the only qualified teammates in MLB history with an ERA+ of 200 or better.
- The Chicago Cubs had five pitchers start twenty or more games in 1907 and every single one of them finished with an ERA below 1.75. Those five pitchers were Jack Pfiester (1.15 ERA), Carl Lundgren (1.17 ERA), Mordecai Brown (1.39 ERA), Orval Overall (1.68 ERA), and Ed Reulbach (1.69 ERA).

No other team in baseball history has ever had four pitchers do this in a season, much less five.

- With a 1.73 earned run average, the Chicago Cubs laid claim to the title for best team ERA in the Modern Era, narrowly beating their 1.75 mark from a year before.
- Nick Maddox, at 20 years and 10 months of age, became (and still remains) the youngest player in MLB history to toss a no-hitter. Maddox finished his age 20 season with a 5-1 record and 0.83 ERA in 54 innings pitched; he's the only player 25 or younger with an ERA that low in 50+ innings in a season in MLB history.
- At the age of 35, Stoney McGlynn became the oldest pitcher to toss 200 innings in his rookie year. He ended up tossing 352.1 innings for the Cardinals in 1907 and would lead the National League in games started, complete games, innings pitched, batters faced, and hits allowed. McGlynn also led the Major Leagues in losses, runs allowed and walks surrendered. McGlynn finished his Major League career the following season totaling just 476.0 innings worth of work.

Honus Wagner led the NL in batting average, slugging percentage, and stolen bases. Few others have showed comparable contact, power, and run tools in the same season as Wagner did in 1907. His .921 OPS may seem unspectacular at first glance, but is put into perspective given the league OPS of .641. (Wagner posted a 187 OPS+.) He'd go on to have even more success in 1908. The 1907 season also saw Ty Cobb become the first player with 200 hits in their age-20 season or younger; only Álex Rodríguez (215 hits in 1996) had more hits in a season at that age.

1908

When most fans think of 1908, they immediately think of the Cubs and the beginning of their all-time long championship drought. It's true. After only winning the National League by a game over both the Giants and Pirates, the 99-55 Cubs knocked off the 90-63 Detroit Tigers four games to one in the World Series. The Cubs would not be World Series champions again for 108 years; they'd defeat the Cleveland Indians in a dramatic seven game World Series in 2016. The Tigers only won the American League by half a game. Neither league's pennant winner was decided until October 6.

Ernie Lombardi, Lefty Gomez, Wes Ferrell, and Al López were born in 1908. Lombardi would be selected to eight NL All Star Teams as a catcher, and also would earn multiple batting titles. Gomez won multiple ERA titles and finished with a perfect 6-0 World Series record for the Yankees (who else?!). Ferrell, who would win 193 games as a pitcher, also hit 38 home runs in 1,176 at bats. Lopez, also a catcher for his entire 19-year career, would get into the Hall of Fame as a 1,410-win manager.

5'7" outfielder Mike Griffin, who stole 94 bases as a rookie in 1887 and led the National League with 36 doubles in 1891, died at age 43. Griffin's 94 stolen bases in 1887 is the second highest single-season total by a player before their 23rd birthday; only Rickey Henderson's 100 stolen bases as a 21-year-old bests Griffin's total.

"Shoeless" Joe Jackson and Frank "Home Run" Baker made their debuts in 1908. Both failed to play even ten games in their first seasons. Shoeless Joe would only get into 30 games total in his first three seasons, making the 1911 season the last in which he qualified as a rookie. Baker would not have as slow a start to his career, playing over 300 games in his first three seasons and leading the American League in triples during his rookie season of 1909.

Joe McGinnity, Jimmy Collins, and Joe Kelley retired following the 1908 season. McGinnity led the National League in wins five times in his ten-year career, along with tossing 17 innings without an earned run in the 1905 World Series. Collins led baseball in home runs in 1898 with 15 long balls and would posthumously be inducted into the Hall of Fame in 1945. Kelley played seventeen seasons in the Majors and his 87 stolen bases in 1896 topped all of baseball.

Chicago Cubs via Wikimedia Commons

Interesting numbers from the 1908 season:

- Honus Wagner's all around dominance continued in 1908. With arguably one of the greatest seasons in MLB history, Wagner led baseball with 201 hits, 39 doubles, 19 triples, 109 RBI, 53 stolen bases, and a .354/.415/.542 slash line. His 11.5 WAR became not only a career high, but a new MLB position player record, topping his 10.2 mark from 1905. No one would surpass this total until Babe Ruth in 1920.
- The Senators' Bob Ganley laid down 52 sacrifice hits in 1908, which would have been good enough to surpass the Major League record of 46, set by Bill Bradley in 1907, but Bradley wound up breaking his own record by putting down

60 sacrifices in 1908. In nine years, Bradley's sacrifice hits record would be broken by Ray Chapman, but his 60 sacrifices in 1908 remains the second-most in a season all time.

- 1908 American League hits leaders:

```
Ty Cobb (DET) - 188
Sam Crawford (DET) - 184
Matty McIntyre (DET) - 168
Nap Lajoie (CLE) - 168
```

- The 3.38 runs per team per game in 1908 is an all-time low in MLB's history, 0.15 runs lower than 1907. The league slugged an all-time worst .305. 1908 is the only year in MLB history in which teams averaged fewer than ten total bases per game.
- Cy Young tossed his third and final no hitter of his career on June 30. His 1.26 ERA in 1908 (at 41 years old) was the best in his career.
- Young became baseball's strikeout king in 1908. With his 2,565th career strikeout, Young passed Tim Keefe for first place on MLB's career strikeout leaderboard. He would hold this title until 1921.
- Ed Walsh's fifteen strikeout outing was topped by Naps starter Addie Joss's perfect game. Joss only struck out three, and the game took 92 minutes to complete.
- Joss's 0.806 WHIP is the third best mark in MLB history by a player with at least 162 innings pitched. Only Pedro Martinez's 0.737 in 2000 and Walter Johnson's 0.780 in 1913 would best Joss's mark. His league leading 1.16 ERA also ranks eighth best by a qualified pitcher all time.
- Walsh did manage to lead baseball with 40 wins, 42 complete

games, eleven shutouts, six saves (unofficial at the time), and 269 strikeouts. He's the only player in MLB history with 40 wins and five saves in a season. His 464 innings pitched make him the most recent pitcher to reach the 400 inning mark in a season.

- Rube Waddell became the first and only player in MLB history to strike out at least 230 hitters and not allow a home run in the same season. While his 7.3 K/9 led the American League for the seventh straight year, he failed to lead the league in strikeouts.

- Waddell's 232 strikeouts in 1908 would tie for the fourth highest single-season total in his career, but with the St. Louis Browns acquiring him during the offseason, he was able to establish a new franchise record for strikeouts in a season. He is still the single-season strikeout leader for the Athletics (349 strikeouts in 1904) and Orioles franchises. He is one of only four pitchers to currently hold the single-season strikeout record for multiple franchises; the others are Nolan Ryan, Randy Johnson, and Pedro Martínez.

- Jim Pastorius went 4-20 with a 2.44 ERA. His .167 W-L% is the worst in MLB history by a pitcher with a sub-3.00 ERA and at least twenty decisions.

- Addie Joss' 1.16 ERA for the Naps not only led the Majors, but it is also a franchise record that no Indians pitcher has ever matched.

- Tigers rookie Ed Summers finished the 1908 season with the eighth-best ERA in the Majors and the fourth-best in the American League, but his 1.64 ERA was good enough to set a Tigers franchise record for the lowest ERA, a record that still stands today. Summers' 145 ERA+ was the highest by a Tigers rookie until 1976, when Mark Fidrych posted a 159

ERA+ in his incredible freshman campaign.

- Earl Moore set the record for most innings pitched in a season without allowing an earned run. He owned a 0.00 ERA in 26 innings.
- In his only big league season, Bill Malarkey made fifteen pitching appearances and totaled 35 innings pitched for the New York Giants. The season in itself is not very noteworthy, but Malarkey did become the first pitcher in MLB history to pitch in ten or more games in a season without making a start. In 2018 there were 298 pitchers who fit that criteria.

1908 was truly the peak of baseball's Dead Ball Era. It produced several incredible pitching seasons that are now nearly impossible to repeat. Honus Wagner overcame the incredible lack of offense, putting together an all-time great offensive season for his Pittsburgh Pirates. In the end, it was the Cubs who would be able to call themselves champions, something they hopefully didn't take for granted.

1909

Finally getting rewarded for his incredible play over the last decade, Honus Wagner and his 110-42 Pittsburgh Pirates won the World Series in seven games over the 98-54 American League Champion Detroit Tigers. Wagner led his Pirates with a .967 OPS in the series, while Fred Clarke hit the team's only two home runs after hitting three in the 152 game regular season. Along with the 104-49 Cubs, it was the first year in National League history with multiple 100 win teams. It wouldn't happen again until 1942.

Mel Ott, Billy Herman, Stan Hack, Dutch Leonard, Mel Harder, Bucky Walters, Claude Passeau, and Lon Warneke were born in 1909. Ott would be selected to eleven consecutive All Star Games, and would rack up all 2,876 of his hits with the Giants. Herman, a second baseman, would lead the NL with 227 hits in 1935. Hack, a teammate of Herman's, won back-to-back stolen base titles in the late 1930s despite finishing with only 33 steals in the two years combined. Leonard, the second player of the same name to play in the Majors, would make five All Star games in his 20-season career. Harder won an ERA title and 223 games in his career, while Walters won the Pitching Triple Crown in 1939 along with another ERA title the next year. Passeau, like Leonard, made five All Star Teams, but failed to lead the league in ERA in any of his 13 seasons. He did, however, tie with Walters for the

NL strikeout title in 1939 with 137. However, ties do count as winners when it comes to the Triple Crown. Warneke would lead the NL in wins and ERA in 1932 for the Cubs.

328 game winner (including 53 in 1885) John Clarkson died at age 47. Clarkson was part of an early days baseball family. His brothers, Arthur and John Clarkson, both had stints as Major League pitchers. His cousins, Mert and Walter Hackett, had even shorter stints in the big leagues as a catcher and a middle infielder respectively.

Zack Wheat and Harry Hooper made their debuts in 1909. Wheat didn't see much playing time for the Brooklyn Superbas in his first season, but he did get the first 31 hits of his career, a career that would see him set the Dodgers franchise record for career hits. Hooper would steal fifteen bases in his first of seventeen big league seasons, and he's just one of six players to swipe at least ten bags in each of his first seventeen seasons. Both Wheat and Hooper would live long enough to see the day that the Veteran's Committees would vote them into Cooperstown.

George Davis and Jack Chesbro retired in 1909. Davis was the first shortstop with 135 RBI in a season and Chesbro led both the National League and American League in seasonal wins within a three-year span (NL in 1902, AL in 1904). Also playing the last game of his career was Arlie Latham, the 1909 season was his first appearances of the 20th century. The 49-year-old Latham was the last player born before the American Civil War to play in a major league game.

Interesting numbers from the 1909 season:

- Bill Bergen's OPS+ of 1 (remember, average is 100) is the worst by a qualified player in MLB history. He hit .139/.163/.156 with one double, one triple, and one home run in 112 games. For perspective, his team's pitchers outhit him with a .160/.197/.216 line, and nineteen extra base hits. Over a nineteen-game span from June 25 to July 19, Bergen went two-for-54.

- Ty Cobb led baseball with nine home runs, all of which were of the inside the park variety. He won the American League Triple Crown with a .377 batting average, those nine homers, and 107 RBI. He also led the league in runs (115), hits (216), stolen bases (76), OBP (.431), and SLG (.517). After Cobb, no Tigers position player would win a Triple Crown until Miguel Cabrera in 2012. Cobb's 25.6 career WAR through his age-22 season is the second most by a position player in MLB history to only Mike Trout (27.7).

- Catcher Billy Sullivan scored eleven runs for the Chicago White Sox. That total represents the fewest scored by an American Leaguer in a qualified season. Sullivan's OPS was a mere .400, so it's not all too difficult to figure out why.

- Fred Clarke became one of two players in MLB history with four walks and an RBI in Game 7 of the World Series. Babe Ruth would follow in his footsteps in 1926.

- The 1909 season is the most recent in which there wasn't a single player with at least ten home runs, and also the most recent in which no pitcher allowed double-digit homers.

- Christy Mathewson's 1.14 ERA in 1909 is the sixth-best by a qualified pitcher in MLB history, and best ever by a Giants pitcher.

- Cubs ace Mordecai Brown completed an MLB record fourth consecutive season with a sub-1.50 ERA. From 1906 to 1909, he went 102-30 with a 1.31 ERA and 32 shutouts in 124 starts.

- Brown's teammate Orval Overall became the second player in MLB history (Christy Mathewson in 1905) with 200 strikeouts and fewer than 50 earned runs allowed in a season. While this feat has become increasingly popular in today's game (four players did it in 2018), only Mathewson, Overall, and Walter Johnson (1913) did it before 1960. Overall, Overall is one of three pitchers in Chicago history to accomplish this feat, along with Chris Sale in 2014 and Jake Arrieta in the following year.
- Teams with 150+ games played and less than 400 runs against:

```
1906 Chicago Cubs
1907 Chicago Cubs
1909 Chicago Cubs
```

- The Cubs never allowed ten runs in a game, and tossed 32 shutouts (over 20% of their games). Their dominance was especially shown against the 45-108 Beaneaters, against whom they went 21-1, with the average game finishing with a score of 6-2.
- Naps shortstop Neal Ball turned an unassisted triple play, the first one in MLB history that is not disputed by historians.

Baseball saw its first winner-take-all postseason game with the Pirates 8-0 demolition of the Tigers in Game 7 of the World Series, the fourth largest run differential in a sudden death World Series game. Bill Bergen would eventually finish his career with -15.0 oWAR, over 5 wins worse than the next lowest mark in MLB history. His -2.6 in 1909 would be his career worst, so in a way, 1909 featured the lowest of lows.

1910

To go along with a fourteen-game increase to the schedule, the 1910 season saw a few rules changes: Major League Baseball optioned to bar team owners from investing in more than one team (this ended syndicate baseball); teams were ordered to deliver their starting lineups to the head umpire at home plate prior to the game; a baserunner would now be called out for passing another baserunner; and umpires were required to announce in-game substitutions to those in attendance. The 104-40 Cubs won the National League pennant, before falling four games to one in the World Series to the 102-48 Philadelphia Athletics. William Howard Taft became the first president to throw out a "first pitch," before Senators ace Walter Johnson one-hit the Athletics.

A pair of great pitchers were born in 1910, Dizzy Dean and Schoolboy Rowe. Dean would become a Hall of Fame pitcher, thanks to his magic on the mound. Schoolboy, on the other hand, would make his way through fifteen seasons as an above-average pitcher and one of baseball's most underrated hitting pitchers of all time.

The year of 1910 also saw the passing of Dan McGann; he would be best remembered as a great defensive first baseman who spent a lot of time getting hit by pitches while at the plate.

Max Carey and Roger Peckinpaugh both make their debuts late in the season. The speedy Carey would go on to play his entire twenty year career in the National League and Peckinpaugh would spend all seventeen of his years in the American League.

Elmer Flick, Addie Joss, Willie Keeler, Sam Leever, Rube Waddell, and Vic Willis would all play in their final games of their careers. All but Leever would eventually be elected into the Hall of Fame, with Keeler being the only one voted in by the BBWAA.

Interesting numbers from the 1910 season:
- April 14th: William Howard Taft became the first US President to throw out a ceremonial first pitch, on Opening Day.
- Jake Stahl of the Boston Red Sox struck out 128 times, giving him the dubious honor of being the hitter with the most strikeouts in a season. It would be his record for 28 years, until Vince DiMaggio's sophomore season of 1938.
- The Chicago White Sox had 25 different players hit a triple in 1910, tying the 1892 Baltimore Orioles' single-season record for the most players on a team with a triple. The White Sox finished the season with 58 triples, good enough for fourteenth place out of the sixteen teams.
- Addie Joss was the sixth and final pitcher to throw a no-hitter during the 1908 season and the first to throw a no-no in 1910. Without a no-hitter being thrown in 1909, Joss became the first of only six pitchers in Major League history to be responsible for consecutive no-hitters on the all time list.
- Between April 28th and September 17th, King Cole of the Chicago Cubs allowed three or fewer runs in each of his 25

starts; those 25 consecutive starts would remain a single-season record until 2018 when the Mets' Jacob deGrom and the Rays' opener Ryne Stanek would string together 29 starts of three runs or fewer. Cole threw 200.0 innings during his stretch, deGrom had 199.1 IP for his streak, and Stanek only tossed 40.0 innings.

- While Ed Walsh led the American League with twenty losses, he also led the Majors with a 1.27 ERA. There have been 482 occurrences in which a pitcher has lost twenty or more games in a season, Walsh's 1.27 ERA is the lowest of all those seasons.
- Ed Walsh's 1.27 ERA is the single-season record for the White Sox franchise. In fact, the club's top three single-season bests were set by Ed Walsh in a three-year span. In 1908, he pitched to a tune of a 1.42 ERA; in 1909, he beat that with a 1.41 mark, only to be bested once again by his 1.27 ERA in 1910.
- Walter Johnson's 313 strikeouts is the single-season record for the Twins franchise. Of the top fifteen strikeout seasons in Twins club history, fourteen belong to one of three pitchers: Walter Johnson with five, Bert Blyleven with five, and Johan Santana with four. Dean Chance's 1968 season in which he struck out 234 is the only one not belonging to one of those three pitchers.
- Jack Coombs' 1.30 ERA is the single-season record for the Athletics franchise. Each of the club's top nine marks were set sometime between 1904 and 1910, with the tenth being set by Vida Blue (1.82 ERA in 1971).
- Coombs recorded thirteen shutouts in 1910. The only other starting pitchers with a baker's dozen in a season? George Bradley (1876), Grover Cleveland Alexander (1916), and Bob Gibson (1968).
- Russ Ford, rookie pitcher for the Highlanders, posted a 1.65

ERA and 0.881 WHIP in 1910. It would take another 106 years until the next rookie would pitch a sub-2.50 ERA and a sub-1.000 WHIP season: José Fernández's 2016 campaign included a 2.19 ERA and a 0.979 WHIP.

- Russ Ford also set an American League rookie record for strikeouts thrown in a season with his 209 punchouts. Herb Score, 245 strikeouts in 1955, and Yu Darvish, 221 strikeouts in 2012, are the only AL rookies to surpass Ford.
- The White Sox's Irv Young won four games on the season, all by way of the shutout. He's the only pitcher to throw 100+ IP in a season and have multiple shutouts that also equaled his win total. He was 4-8 (.333) that year.

The 1910 season began with William Howard Taft becoming the first United States President to throw out a ceremonial first pitch; it ended with one of the greatest controversies in the history of baseball. Before the season started, Hugh Chalmers of Chalmers Automobile Company promised to award the batting champs for each league with one of his Chalmers Model 30 automobiles. With a couple days left in the season, Ty Cobb was leading Nap Lajoie .385 to .377 for the AL batting title and riding a fourteen-game hitting streak to boot. Cobb opted to sit out the last two games of the season believing the Model 30 could only be lost by him and not won by Lajoie. With one day left and a doubleheader against the last place Browns still on the schedule, Nap would need a perfect day to surpass Cobb. Thanks to some help from Jack O'Connor, the Browns' manager, playing his third baseman on the outfield grass, Nap would go four-for-four in the first game. O'Connor, who was known to dislike Ty Cobb, continued to play his third baseman back during the second game as well. Lajoie was also four-for-four in the second game and looking for his 7th bunt single on the day when his last bunt was officially scored as a sacrifice hit after it was misplayed and ruled as a fielding error.

Lajoie would finish the season with a .384 batting average, but only after Browns coach Harry Howell unsuccessfully tried to bribe the official scorer into changing the error to a hit on Nap's last at bat. Major League Baseball would name Cobb as the official batting champ and then proceed to ban O'Connor and Howell from the league for their roles on that final day. As for the big prize, Chalmers would end up giving both Cobb and Lajoie one of his Model 30 vehicles, pretty much declaring it a tie.

The story doesn't end there, though. Fast forward 68 years to 1978 when sabermetrician Pete Palmer discovers that Ty Cobb's 1910 season statistics contained a double-counted box score; this mistake allowed for an extra 2 for 3 game to be counted and changed a .382 season into a .385 season. All that, and there's yet another layer to this story. It appears that the league office had already found this mistake back in 1910, because all the other Detroit Tigers (who were not named Ty Cobb) had their statistics updated without the extra game included.

1911

While the sixteen teams in Major League Baseball remained the same, the Boston Doves became the Rustlers and the Brooklyn Superbas became the Trolley Dodgers, or Dodgers for short. The two teams finished in last and second to last in the National League, respectively. Meanwhile, the New York Giants won the NL pennant at 99-54, before falling victim to the 101-50 Athletics in the World Series that earned John Baker the nickname "Home Run." The A's became the second team in World Series history with back-to-back titles (also the Cubs in 1907 and 1908). On June 28, the new Polo Grounds opened for business.

Hall of Famers Hank Greenberg, Joe Medwick, and Walter Alston were born in 1911. Greenberg's 1.017 OPS ranks sixth all time. Alston batted only once as a player, but managed the Dodgers from 1954 to 1976. Hall of Fame Negro Leaguer Josh Gibson was also born in 1911. While some called him the "black Babe Ruth," some who saw them both play dubbed Ruth "the white Josh Gibson." His Hall of Fame plaque credits him with nearly 800 home runs in his pro baseball career.

Addie Joss and Bob Caruthers died in 1911. Joss, allowed a total of 2,252 walks and hits in 2,327.0 innings in his career, giving him an MLB best 0.968 career WHIP. Caruthers went 218-99 in his career, and also led the American Association with a 201 OPS+ in 1886.

Grover Cleveland "Pete" Alexander made his debut in 1911, leading baseball with 28 wins and seven shutouts.

Cy Young capped off an all-time great career in 1911 with a 7-9 record in eighteen starts. He has the most starts, wins, losses, complete games, innings pitched, hits allowed, earned runs allowed, and pitching WAR in MLB history. He never had an opportunity to win the award named after him, but his name will always be cemented in baseball history thanks in part to the award.

Interesting numbers from the 1911 season:
- The Phillies began a record setting streak of 62 consecutive Opening Day games without being shut out. It's the longest such streak in MLB history.
- Ty Cobb's .420 batting average was 145 points better than the MLB position player average of .275. It's the biggest differential between a player's and the league's batting average since 1901.
- A .420 batting average is definitely not easy to obtain, but setting a new mark for consecutive games with a hit would help tremendously. Cobb did just that by recording a hit in 40 straight games from May 15th through July 2nd. He averaged exactly two hits per game and slashed a ridiculous .476/.514/.661 during his streak. It would remain the longest hit streak in the Majors for more than eleven years.
- Cobb's 248 hits became a new MLB record, topping Jesse Burkett's record mark of 240 set in 1896. Cobb did so in only

146 games; his hit total translates to a 162 game pace of 275 hits. Only three AL players: George Sisler, Al Simmons, and Ichiro, have topped Cobb's 248 hit season. Ichiro's 262 hits in 2004 are an MLB record, but he only managed 37 extra base hits compared to Cobb's 79.

- Cobb's 1911 season is the only in MLB history with 75 extra base hits and 75 stolen bases.
- Cobb also set a Tigers franchise record with 147 runs scored in a season. Only one Detroit player has even scored 120 runs this century; that was Curtis Granderson's 122 in 2007.
- Frank Schulte's 21 homers led all of baseball. He also became the only player in MLB history with twenty doubles, triples, homers, and stolen bases, and 100 runs batted in a single season. Wait, you didn't get this book for extremely specific stats like that one?
- Shoeless Joe Jackson's .408 batting average is the best by a rookie in MLB history. Although he debuted in 1908, he was still considered a rookie in 1911 because of how few games he played in from 1908-1910. No Cleveland player has topped Jackson's 1911 batting average.
- Jackson's 233 hits are the second most ever by a rookie, behind only Ichiro's historic 2001 season in which he had 242 hits in his first season in the United States. His 1.058 OPS is also a rookie record, 9 points ahead of Aaron Judge's 2017 season.
- Shoeless Joe narrowly edged out Cobb for MLB's on-base percentage title, .468 to .466. The two each topped 9.0 WAR, while no other position player even managed to reach the 7.0 mark. Shoeless Joe's .468 OBP is still the highest mark by a rookie in Major League history.
- Cubs left fielder Jimmy Sheckard set an MLB record by drawing 147 walks in the 1911 season. The previous record

was 136 set by the man Jack Crooks in 1892. Sheckard led the NL with a .434 OBP despite a mere .276 average.

- 1911 is the only season of record in which there were multiple batters with 230+ hits (Ty Cobb and Shoeless Joe Jackson) and multiple pitchers with 230+ strikeouts (Ed Walsh, Rube Marquard, and Smoky Joe Wood).

- After scoring thirteen runs in the first inning, New York Giants manager John McGraw decided to preserve his starter, Christy Mathewson, by replacing him with Rube Marquard. Marquard then set a relief pitcher record with fourteen strikeouts in the eight innings he pitched. His record was topped only a couple of years later by Walter Johnson, when he struck out fifteen in 11.1 relief innings.

- Buck O'Brien's 0.38 ERA in 47.2 IP gave him MLB's best ERA among all pitchers with at least 30 innings in a season.

- The Detroit Tigers set a post-19th Century record by winning 21 of their first 23 games. The 1955 Dodgers are the only other team to do that.

- The Tigers set another record by rallying from a twelve-run deficit to defeat the White Sox 16-15 on June 18. Detroit fell behind 13-1 heading into the bottom of the fifth inning, but scored 15 runs in the next five frames while holding Chicago to only a two-run seven inning.

After leading the American League in most offensive stats (besides home runs) and setting the MLB hit record, Ty Cobb took home the league's Chalmers Award. Meanwhile, Frank Schulte won the NL's award after hitting an MLB best 21 home runs and NL best 107 RBI and 308 total bases. While they didn't award a Rookie of the Year award quite yet, it's safe to give MLB's all-time Rookie of the Year award to Shoeless Joe Jackson's historic 1911 season.

1912

1912 saw the opening of three historic ballparks: Navin Field, which would eventually become Tiger Stadium; Redland Field, which would become Crosley Field; and the still standing Fenway Park. 1912 also marked the first year in which Earned Run Average, or ERA, was officially kept by the National League. ERA is calculated by finding the average amount of earned runs allowed by a pitcher per 9 innings. The Boston Rustlers became the Braves, which they would keep through the present day, besides the years 1936-1940 when they were known as the Bees. With Fenway Park as their new home, 105-47 Red Sox won the World Series 4-3-1 over the 103-48 New York Giants; Game 2 was declared a tie. The Red Sox also became the first team to come within an inning of losing the Series to come back and win it all. That would not happen again until 1986.

Nine-time All Star Arky Vaughan was born in 1912. Vaughan played 722 games at shortstop through his age-24 season and sported a .925 OPS during that time. Of the 189 shortstops to have played 200+ games at the position before their age-25 season, only Álex Rodríguez carried a higher OPS than Vaughan. Á-Rod slashed .309/.374/.561 during his first seven seasons, good enough for a .934 OPS.

Cupid Childs, owner of one of the best names in baseball history and totaler of 44.3 WAR from 1888 to 1901, died at age 45. He and Lou Gehrig remain the only infielders to total 135+ runs scored in three consecutive seasons. Childs accomplished the feat from 1892-1894, while Lou Gehrig had two such streaks, with the first being from 1926-1928 and the second extending four seasons from 1930-1933.

Players to debut in 1912 include Stan Coveleski, Eppa Rixey, Wilbur Cooper, Heinie Groh, Bobby Veach, Del Pratt, Herb Pennock, and Rabbit Maranville. Coveleski started only two games for the Athletics, and would not play again in the Majors until 1916. Rixey would toss 162 innings for the Phillies; he'd throw at least 100 in every year until 1933, except for in 1918 when he was serving in the Great War. Cooper started his fifteen year career with a 3-0 season, and a 1.66 ERA in 38 innings. Groh batted 56 times for the Giants as a second baseman; he'd later move to Cincinnati and play the hot corner. Veach played 23 games for Detroit, where he hit .342 in his first of what would be a dozen seasons in Motor City. Pratt had an interesting season, playing 152 games, stealing 24 bases but getting caught 30 times. He'd lead the AL in games in each year from 1913 to 1916. Pennock, 18 at the time, debuted as a reliever for Philadelphia; the future Hall of Famer posted a 4.50 ERA in his first season. Maranville, also a future Hall of Famer, went 18-for-86 for the Braves in his debut season.

Jack Powell, loser of double-digit games in each of his sixteen career seasons, retired following the 1912 season. He went 9-17 in his final season, and finished his career with a 245-255 record. Powell is the only player in baseball history to rack up 55+

pitching WAR in his career and still finish with a losing record.

Interesting numbers from the 1912 season:
- With 226 hits and 61 stolen bases, Ty Cobb became the only player in MLB history with multiple seasons of 225 hits and 50 stolen bases. It was the second year in a row Cobb had done this; he would do it for a third time in 1917. It was also the third of what would be an MLB-best seven seasons with at least 200 hits and 50 stolen bases. The only other player with three such seasons in their career is Lou Brock. Cobb had done it three times before turning 25 years old.
- Tris Speaker became the first player in MLB history with 50 doubles and 50 stolen bases in a season. Only Craig Biggio in 1998 would join him. Speaker also led the American League in home runs and on-base percentage.
- Speaker also had a 30 game hit streak and two 20 game hit streaks in 1912. In the 70 games encompassed by those streaks, Speaker batted .424 with 118 hits and 68 runs scored.
- Despite racking up *only* 37 triples from 1909 to 1911, Pirates outfielder Chief Wilson set a still-standing MLB record with 36 triples in one season, topping the previous record of 31 that was set in 1886. Wilson is also the only player in the 20th or 21st century with a triple in five consecutive games. In the five games from June 17 to June 20, he racked up seven hits: one single and six triples. That's a lot of running.
- No one since has topped Shoeless Joe Jackson's .480 home batting average in 1912. He went 130 for 271 in games played in Cleveland.
- The White Sox's Ed Walsh struck out 254 batters. It would be the fourth and final time that he'd reach the 250-strikeout mark in a season. The only American League pitchers with

more such seasons are Nolan Ryan and Roger Clemens, they have seven and five such seasons respectively.

- Walter Johnson's 1912 season is one of four seasons in MLB history with 300 strikeouts and an ERA+ of 200 or better. The other three times this has been accomplished were Old Hoss Radbourn in 1884, and Pedro Martinez in 1997 and 1999. Through six seasons, Johnson owned a 1.69 career ERA and 1,218 strikeouts.

- With 14.3 Wins Above Replacement, Johnson led the American League in WAR for the first of what would be five consecutive seasons. The only other players in MLB history to lead their league in WAR in five seasons in a row are Babe Ruth and Mike Trout.

- Walter Johnson and Bob Groom both eclipsed 175 strikeouts on the season for the Washington Senators. It would take exactly another 100 years before the next time a set of teammates reached that mark while playing for a team in the nation's capital. Gio González and Stephen Strasburg would strike out 207 and 197 hitters, respectively, for the 2012 Washington Nationals.

- Red Sox ace Smoky Joe Wood went 34-5. His .872 Win-Loss% is the best in a season in MLB history with more than 35 decisions. Wood also started three games and closed another one in the World Series. He went 3-1 in the Series, including a three-inning relief appearance in Game 8. He allowed the go ahead run in the tenth inning, but his Red Sox scored two runs in the bottom of the tenth to secure Boston the title and Wood the victory.

- On July 4, George Mullin became the first (and only pitcher so far) to toss a no hitter on their birthday.

- The St. Louis Browns reached the century mark in losses for the third consecutive season. The 1910-1912 Browns are the sole MLB team to have a team ERA below 4.00 three years in a row and still lose 100+ games.

With eight players racking up at least 8.5 WAR, there was no easy choice for the Chalmers Award in the American League. In the end, it was awarded to Tris Speaker and his 50 double/50 stolen base season. His 1.031 OPS ranked third and his 10.1 WAR ranked fourth, but first among position players. In the National League, Larry Doyle took home the award, despite placing ninth in WAR at 5.0. The Giants second baseman batted .330 with ten home runs. In the end, it was Speaker's Red Sox who reigned victorious with a World Series win and a new, familiar ballpark.

1913

Baseball saw new nicknames for two of its most prolific franchises, with the New York Highlanders becoming the Yankees and the Brooklyn Trolley Dodgers shortening their name to the Dodgers. Okay, well quick aside here: the legal name for the Dodgers was the Brooklyn Base Ball Club. The nicknames we've used (like Bridegrooms, Grooms, Ward's Wonder's, Superbas, and even (Trolley) Dodgers) were unofficial nicknames used by writers to talk about the team. Many were used interchangeably, and the term "Dodgers" wasn't seen on a uniform until 1932. Until then, you might see them referred to as the Superbas, Dodgers, or Robins. They all are referring to the same team. Anyway, the Dodgers played their first season at the historic Ebbets Field in 1913; they'd play there until their move to Los Angeles. For the third time in four years, the Philadelphia Athletics (96-57) captured the World Series title, this time four games to one over the 101-51 New York Giants. The Athletics are one of three franchises to have won three World Series in a four-year span, along with the Red Sox (who did it later this decade), and the Yankees (who did it quite often). The St. Louis Browns and Cardinals finished in last place in their respective leagues.

Future Hall of Fame first baseman Johnny Mize was born in 1913. He would go on to lead the NL in OPS in three consecutive seasons, then join the Navy for three years, and then go on to win five championships in a row with the Yankees in his final five big league seasons.

Red Donahue, baseball's most recent 35-game loser in 1897, died in 1913 at the young age of 40 years old. Donahue had his best seasons of his career from 1901 to 1904, totaling 124 complete games and a 76-54 (.585) record. Only five pitchers finished with more complete games and a greater Win-Loss% during that span; Jack Chesbro, Christy Mathewson, Joe McGinnity, Rube Waddell, and Cy Young. All five of those guys have plaques in Cooperstown.

Bob Shawkey, Edd Roush, and Wally Schang debuted in 1913. Shawkey went 6-5 with a 2.34 ERA for the Athletics in his rookie season, while Schang, one of their catchers, posted a .392 OBP in 254 PA. Roush went one-for-ten in his short stint with the White Sox.

Jimmy Sheckard and Doc White retired in 1913. Only seven players have finished their careers with more hits, walks, and stolen bases than Sheckard. Of those seven players, Barry Bonds is the only one yet to be inducted into the Hall of Fame. White played eleven of his thirteen big league seasons for the Chicago White Sox, racking up over 1,000 strikeouts and 159 wins. Only his teammate Ed Walsh, Mark Buehrle, and Chris Sale put up more strikeouts and a better win-loss record in a Sox uniform than the great Doc White.

Shoeless Joe Jackson via Wikimedia Commons

Interesting numbers from the 1913 season:
- With first baseman Stuffy McInnis, second baseman Eddie Collins, shortstop Jack Barry, and third baseman Home Run Baker, the Athletics became one of two teams with an entire infield of 4.5 WAR players. The 1898 Orioles were the others.
- Senators outfielder Clyde Milan followed up his 1912 season in which he batted .306 and stole 88 bases with a .301/75 season. Milan is one of two players in American League history with back-to-back seasons of a .300 batting average and 75 stolen bases. Can you guess the other? Here's a hint: it's not Rickey Henderson or Ty Cobb; it's actually Willie

Wilson, who did it in 1979 and 1980 for the Royals.

- Phillies right fielder Gavvy Cravath led baseball with nineteen home runs. It'd be the first of three consecutive seasons he would lead the National League in home runs. In fact, of the five players to lead the NL in homers three times in a row, three were Phillies (also Chuck Klein and Mike Schmidt).

- In his third full season, Naps outfielder Joe Jackson had his third 1.000 OPS season. From 1911 to 1913, Jackson batted .393/.462/.574, good for an OPS+ of 192.

- Teammates Eddie Collins, Home Run Baker, Eddie Murphy, and Rube Oldring all cross the plate more than 100 times apiece in 1913. For the first two decades of the 20th century, these Athletics are the only foursome to all reach 100 runs scored in the same season.

- Unfortunately for Giants outfielder George Burns, 1913 just so happens to be one of the seasons with available caught stealing data. Not only did Burns lead the Majors with 35 caught stealings, he also led the NL with 74 strikeouts at the plate.

- Pitcher Frank Allen went 4-18 with a 2.83 ERA. His .182 W-L% is the second-lowest ever for a pitcher with a sub-3.00 ERA and at least 20 decisions. That "record" belongs to Jim Pastorius, who went 4-20 with a 2.44 ERA in 1908. Both Allen and Pastorius played for Brooklyn.

- Walter Johnson got off to an historic start to the 1913 season. In the first month of the season, he appeared in five games, tossing four complete games and recording a one inning save, only allowing one run. He owned a 0.24 ERA for the month. He went three more games without allowing an earned run; as of May 13th he had a 7-0 record with a save, and a 0.17 ERA in 53.2 innings pitched.

- Johnson finished the year with one of the best pitching seasons of all time:

```
36-7 (best Win-Loss% ever, minimum 40 decisions)
1.14 ERA (fourth best ever, minimum 150 IP; best
    ever, minimum 325 IP)
0.780 WHIP (second best ever to Pedro Martinez's
    2000, minimum 150 IP)
259 ERA+ (fifth best ever, minimum 150 IP; best
    ever, minimum 325 IP)
```

- Johnson's 1.14 ERA is also the best in Twins franchise history. In fact, he owns ten of the top eleven Twins/Senators seasons (the other belonging to Bill Burns and his 1.70 ERA in 1908).
- Johnson's 15.1 pitching WAR is the most ever by a post-19th Century pitcher, topping his 13.2 mark from the previous season. That's more pitching WAR in two seasons than Trevor Hoffman had in his entire Hall of Fame career!
- Christy Mathewson (25 wins, 21 walks) became the first Modern Era pitcher with 25+ wins and fewer than 25 walks allowed in a season. No one since has joined him.
- A 23-year-old lefty named Slim Love made his Major League debut for the Washington Senators on September 8, 1913. He'd throw a clean ninth inning against the New York Yankees in a 4-0 defeat. None of that was of much importance to Slim Love's place in the record books, but the fact that the towering pitcher stood 6 foot 7 inches (201 cm) was of importance. Love's debut made him the tallest player to play in MLB's first 38 seasons.

1913 was all about Walter Johnson. He had an all-time great pitching season, and even was an above average hitter as evidenced by his .261 batting average and 109 OPS+. His 16.4 WAR (as a hitter and pitcher) led baseball by over seven wins. He became the first pitcher ever to win the Chalmers Award, while Brooklyn's Jake Daubert took home the award in the NL with a .350 batting average and 25 stolen bases. His 4.0 WAR was over twelve wins worse than Johnson's. Neither player led his team to a World Series win; it was the Athletics star-studded infield that brought the title back to Philly for the third time in four years.

1914

In 1914, the Federal League is recognized as a third Major League, which played opposite the American League and National League in 1914 and 1915. With star players such as Joe Tinker and Mordecai Brown, the eight team FL drew respectable crowds. The Indianapolis Hoosiers paced the new Major League at 88-65, followed by the Chicago Chi-Feds, Baltimore Terrapins, Buffalo Buffeds, Brooklyn Tip-Tops, Kansas City Packers, Pittsburgh Rebels, and St. Louis Terriers. Chicago played at Weeghman Park, which would later be known as Wrigley Field. The Philadelphia Athletics once again won the American League pennant, but got swept in the World Series by the Boston Braves. The Brooklyn team was now known as the Robins in 1914.

Future Hall of Famer Joe DiMaggio was born on November 25, 1914. DiMaggio would be best known for his record 56 game hitting streak and nine World Series championships.

Rube Waddell, the six-time AL strikeout champion and 1905 Pitching Triple Crown winner, died of tuberculosis at the age of 37. We recommend Googling Rube Waddell to learn all the incredible stories about him. This book just isn't really the place for them, unfortunately.

19-year-old pitcher Babe Ruth made his debut for the Boston Red Sox in 1914. He had a 3.91 ERA in 23.0 IP, and went two-for-ten at the dish. Also making debuts were Harry Heilmann (.629 OPS in 217 PA), Red Faber (2.68 ERA in 181.1 IP), Dolf Luque (four ER in 8.2 IP), and Sad Sam Jones (one ER in 3.1 IP).

Frank Chance and Clark Griffith played their final stints in the Majors in 1914. Griffith pitched in a grand total of eight innings from 1908 to 1914, but won an ERA title at the tail end of the 19th century and managed to pitch an inning in 1914. Chance, a key part of the 1907 and 1908 World Series Champion Cubs, was a player/manager for the Yankees in his final year in the big leagues. Chance used himself as a player just once in 1914, entering the fourth game of the season as a pinch runner and staying in the game to play first base afterwards. He wouldn't get a plate appearance in his final game.

Interesting numbers from the 1914 season:
- 1914 featured the first two players to reach the 3,000 hit mark since Cap Anson became its inaugural member back in 1897. On June 9, Honus Wagner racked up his 3,000th, while Nap Lajoie joined the club on September 27.
- Federal League rookie outfielder Benny Kauff led all of baseball with 211 hits, 75 stolen bases, a .370 average, and a .981 OPS. He and Ichiro (2001) are the only rookies in MLB history with 200 hits and 50 stolen bases in a season. Kauff is the only one with 200 and 75. Over a 60 game span from May 6 to July 16, Kauff maintained a .404 batting average and 1.101 OPS.
- Gavvy Cravath led baseball in home runs for the second season in a row with nineteen. This year, all of his homers

came at his home field (the Baker Bowl), where he hit .300/.423/.601. On the road he hit .295/.375/.384. The Baker Bowl was one of the most hitter friendly parks in baseball history; Cravath hit 92 of his 119 career home runs at the Baker Bowl despite only taking 44% of his career plate appearances there.

- Home Run Baker's nine home runs in 1914 was good enough to lead the American League in round trippers for the second consecutive season. Baker and Cravath became the first pair of hitters to outright lead the AL and NL in home runs in the same consecutive seasons. They have since been joined on this list by George Foster and Jim Rice for their 1977 and 1978 seasons and by Mark McGwire and Ken Griffey Jr. for the damage that they did during the 1998 and 1999 seasons.

- Reds outfielder George Twombly set an MLB record by hitting five triples, but no doubles or homers. That's still the most extra base hits, all coming from triples, in a season in MLB history. He would finish his career with one double, seven triples, and zero home runs.

- Outfielder Doc Miller scored just eight runs in 93 games for the 1914 Cincinnati Reds. He and the infamous Bill Bergen are the only players to score that few runs in a qualified season. Bergen scored eight times in 99 games in 1908 for the Brooklyn Superbas.

- 22-year-old Dutch Leonard's 0.96 ERA made him one of two qualified players in MLB history with an ERA below 1.00 (Tim Keefe in 1880 being the other). Leonard is the only player to do it with at least 150 innings pitched. He amazingly did not surrender more than six earned runs in any stretch of six games. Keep in mind, he was a starting pitcher; he started 25 of the 36 games he played in and averaged over 6 innings per appearance.

- When it was all said and done, Leonard pitched ten seasons with at least 125 innings pitched in his career. After his 0.96 mark, Leonard's next best season in terms of ERA was 2.17, over 1.2 runs worse than his historic 1914 season.

- After finishing the season with a 17-3 record, Athletics starter Chief Bender now had three seasons in his career with at least seventeen wins and no more than five losses. The only other pitchers with three such seasons in their career are Roger Clemens, Randy Johnson, and Clayton Kershaw.

- Hooks Wiltse appeared on the mound twenty times in 1914, a mark that Wiltse had reached nine times before, but what made this season special was the fact that he didn't start any of those twenty games. This made the Giants pitcher the first person to toss 20+ games in a season without a start, something Giants manager John McGraw would get out of six different pitchers over a twelve-year span. By the end of 1925, the New York Giants were responsible for six of the ten seasons in which a pitcher finished the year with 20+ relief appearances and no starts.

In his first year in Boston, Johnny Evers took home the NL Chalmers Award with the Braves. His .338 slugging percentage is the worst by an MVP position player in MLB history (he was an excellent defender at second base and got on base at a .390 clip, however). In the AL, fellow second baseman Eddie Collins took home the Chalmers Award with a .344 average and .452 OBP. It would be Collins' final season in Philadelphia until 1927.

1915

Now known as the Chicago Whales, the Joe Tinker-managed Federal League club barely won the pennant over the St. Louis Terriers and Pittsburgh Rebels. It'd be the second and final season of the Federal League's MLB stint. After releasing most of their talent, the Philadelphia Athletics went from first to worst in the American League, finishing the season with a 43-109 record. The AL Pennant would go to the 101-50 Boston Red Sox, who would defeat the 90-62 Philadelphia Phillies in five games in the World Series. Both clubs declined a challenge from the Whales to play in an inter-league playoff. Meanwhile, with the aging Nap Lajoie purchased by the Athletics, Cleveland chose the "Indians" as the nickname to replace the "Naps," which had previously been chosen to honor Lajoie.

Future Hall of Famer Joe Gordon was born in February of 1915. He was the first of just three players to play 100+ games at second base and total 50 or more extra base hits in each of his first six seasons in the Major Leagues. He would later be joined on this short list by Robinson Canó and Dan Uggla.

Ross Barnes and Al Spalding, two of the pivotal players of the early years of the National League, died in 1915. Barnes, if you recall from the first subchapter of this book, hit .429 in 1876.

Spalding led the NL with 47 wins in 1876, in addition to leading the National Association in wins in each of its five seasons. Tip O'Neill, the Canada-born outfielder that batted .435 in 1887, and American Association star Dave Orr also died in 1915.

Rogers Hornsby, Dazzy Vance, George Sisler, Sam Rice, Carl Mays, Dave Bancroft, and High Pockets Kelly debuted in 1915. Hornsby, the greatest second baseman of all time, went 14-for-57 with the St. Louis Cardinals in his first season. Vance, 24, wouldn't actually win a game until his 30s; he went 0-4 in 1915 at age 24. Sisler batted .285 for the St. Louis Browns and also started eight games on the mound, finishing with a 2.83 ERA. Rice, in his first of nineteen seasons with the Washington Senators, batted only eight times, racking up three singles. He also pitched eighteen innings, allowing only four earned runs. Mays led the Majors by closing 27 games for the Boston Red Sox in 1915, and didn't allow a single homer. Bancroft, the Phillies shortstop, went a staggering 15 for 42... on stolen base attempts in 1915. He also hit seven home runs. Kelly, the nephew of 1897 stolen base leader Bill Lange, played 17 games for the Giants in his first season.

Fred Clarke, Roger Bresnahan, and George Mullin retired after 1915. Clarke had not been a full-time player since 1911, when he posted a .900 OPS. Bresnahan, the ole' catcher slash center fielder, retired with a .386 career on-base percentage. Mullin posted a 101 ERA+ in 3,686.2 career innings, mostly for Detroit, and remains the only American League pitcher to lead the league in walks allowed for four consecutive years.

Interesting numbers from the 1915 season:
- Ty Cobb won the American League batting title for the

ninth consecutive season. While his 1910 batting average is disputed due to subsequent research, the batting title is permanent and thus gives him boldface text on his Baseball-Reference page despite Lajoie having the better average, according to the site. Anyways, the nine consecutive batting titles that Cobb won from 1907-1915 are more than any other player in MLB history has won in their entire career. Cobb could've retired after 1915, still in his 20s, and he would still have the most batting titles in baseball history. He didn't, however, and would finish his career with a dozen.

- From 1907 to 1915, a nine-year span, Cobb racked up a ridiculous 1,786 hits and 559 stolen bases. For comparison, Johnny Evers, winner of the NL Chalmers Award in 1914, played in parts of 18 seasons and totaled 1,659 hits and 324 stolen bases. Evers, as well as his teammates Joe Tinker and Frank Chance, all fell short of Cobb's nine year stats over their careers but all would later be inducted into the Baseball Hall of Fame.

- Cobb also stole a career high 96 bases and drew a career high 118 walks in 1915. He's one of three players (Billy Hamilton 1894, Rickey Henderson 1980 and 1982) with 90 stolen bases and 110 walks drawn in a season.

- Honus Wagner's 5.6 WAR is the second most ever by a position player in his 40s, behind only Willie Mays' 6.3 in 1971. Wagner was 41, and Mays was only 40, so Wagner has the single-season record for all players 41 or older. The only pitchers 41 or older to match Wagner's 5.6 WAR: Cy Young, Roger Clemens, Randy Johnson, Dennis Martinez, Warren Spahn.

- Gavvy Cravath's 24 home runs were, at the time, the fourth most in a season and most in a season in the 20th century.

Nineteen of his 24 were hit at the Baker Bowl. Cravath became the first player to lead baseball in home runs in three consecutive seasons; only Babe Ruth, Ralph Kiner, Mike Schmidt, and Mark McGwire have done so since.

- Honus Wagner passed Cap Anson for first place all time on the career total base list. He finished the year with 4,640 total bases to his name. Anson had possessed the record since 1881.
- There were 62 players that finished the 1915 season with at least ten triples. That's two more than the number of players that have hit double-digit triples in a season in the seventeen years from 2002 to 2018.
- 1915 saw an MLB record 4,441 sacrifice hits, including five players with at least 40.
- To go along with his NL pitching Triple Crown, Grover Cleveland (Pete) Alexander became one of three pitchers in National League history with an ERA+ of 225 or better and at least 225 strikeouts in a season. The other two? Bob Gibson in 1968 and Dwight Gooden in 1985.
- Pete Alexander's 1.22 ERA broke George McQuillan's Phillies franchise-record 1.53 ERA that he set seven years earlier, in 1908. His 1.22 ERA remains the Phillies' lowest ERA in a season by a qualified pitcher. Alexander's 1916 and 1917 seasons rank third and fourth on the list, respectively.
- On June 17, Cubs pitcher Zip Zabel came out of the bullpen with two outs in the first inning. He would end up pitching the rest of the nineteen inning game, finishing with a relief pitcher record 18.1 innings pitched in one game. He earned the hard fought victory, allowing only two runs.
- 56 players saw the field for the Athletics in 1915, the most by a team in a season in the Dead Ball Era.

- The Philadelphia Athletics used 24 starting pitchers (27 total pitchers). That's four more starters than any other team in MLB history has ever used in a single season. All 27 of their pitchers were 27 years of age or younger, 26 of them were 26 years of age or younger, and 25 of them were playing in their age-25 season or earlier! All of those are records.

Unfortunately, the Chalmers Award was discontinued following the 1914 season; there wouldn't be another award similar to the MVP award we have today until 1922. Grover Cleveland Alexander likely would have won the NL's version, however, as his 1915 season is one of twelve in baseball history to qualify for the MLB Pitching Triple Crown (leading not only one league, but all of baseball, in wins, ERA, and strikeouts). Also in 1915, Ty Cobb kept doing his thing.

1916

In their first year in the recently constructed ballpark on the North Side of Chicago that would later be called Wrigley Field, the Cubs didn't find much success, finishing the season with an unimpressive 67-86 record. The Cubs did become the first team to allow fans to keep baseballs hit into the stands though. The National League saw a huge split between the top half and bottom half of the standings. 19.5 games seperated the fourth place Giants (86-66) and the fifth place Cubs, while there was a mere 7 game difference between both first and fourth, and fifth and last. The 94-60 Brooklyn Robins secured the pennant in the competitive National League, but fell in five games to the 91-63 Boston Red Sox. The two franchises would not meet in the World Series again until 2018.

Enos Slaughter, Bob Elliot, and Charlie Keller were born in 1916. Slaughter would make ten consecutive All Star Games, besides the three years he spent serving in World War II. Elliott would win an MVP award in 1947, posting a .927 OPS with the Braves that year. Keller would win three World Series titles with the Yankees, including their 1939 sweep in which he posted a 1.858 OPS.

Dick McBride, one of the most successful National Association pitchers during the 5 years the league existed, passed away in 1916 at the age of 68. He ranks second in wins, third in innings pitched, and fourth in strikeouts in National Association history. McBride played all five of his NA seasons with the Philadelphia Athletics and would retire after pitching in just four games for the Boston Beaneaters in the inaugural season of the National League in 1876.

Urban Shocker and Burleigh Grimes made their debuts in 1916. Shocker started nine games for the Yankees, while Grimes started five for Pittsburgh.

1916 marked the end of the careers of several Hall of Fame players. Nap Lajoie, owner of the best single-season batting average in American League history (.426 in 1901) capped off his 3,000+ hit career with 105 more in 1916. Hall of Famers Joe Tinker and Mordecai Brown, both important pieces to the first two Cubs' World Series, both ended their careers with Chicago. Two time Triple Crown Winner Christy Mathewson played his first 635 career games with the Giants, but his final game came with Cincinnati in what happened to be both his and longtime rival Mordecai Brown's last Major League appearance. Both went the distance, but Mathewson's eight runs allowed actually netted him the victory, as Three Finger Brown allowed ten. Hall of Famer Miller Huggins also retired after a thirteen season career in which he did not play an inning at any position besides second base.

Interesting numbers from the 1916 season:
- On September 8, Wally Schang became the first player in MLB history to homer from both sides of the plate in a game.
- Ty Cobb did not lead the AL in any slash stat for the first

time in a decade. Cleveland's Tris Speaker led baseball in all three stats at .386/.470/.502, with Cobb finishing second in average and OBP, and third in SLG. He did still lead the game with 113 runs and 68 stolen bases.

- Bert Niehoff posted a .356 SLG despite leading the Majors with 42 doubles. The Phillies second baseman also racked up four triples and four home runs. His .356 slugging percentage is the lowest in a season in MLB history by a player with at least 50 extra base hits. The next lowest mark belongs to Jose Bautista's 2017 season in which he slugged .366 despite 27 doubles and 23 dingers.
- Gavvy Cravath became the first player in MLB history with five consecutive double-digit home run seasons.
- In 323.2 IP, Red Sox southpaw Babe Ruth led the American League in ERA and failed to allow a home run, all while hitting three at the plate in 152 plate appearances. However, the Major League record for most innings in a season without allowing a home run belongs to Walter Johnson and his 1916 campaign, in which he tossed 369.2 IP without ceasing a dinger. He hit one himself.
- Grover Cleveland (Pete) Alexander tied George Bradley's single-season record with sixteen shutouts. Bradley's total had been the record ever since the National League's inaugural season in 1876. The two remain co-owners of the record today.
- As a result of twelve shutouts from 1915 paired with an even more spectacular season, Alexander also became the only pitcher in MLB history with consecutive double-digit shutout seasons. To put into perspective how ridiculous 28 shutouts in a two-year span is, consider the following: as of the writing of this book in 2018, Pedro Martinez and Clayton Kershaw

have combined for 32 career shutouts.

- Runs allowed in Alexander's starts from 1915 to 1916:

```
0: 28 starts (Philadelphia was 28-0)
1: 13 starts (Philadelphia was 11-1-1)
2: 16 starts (Philadelphia was 11-5)
3: 12 starts (Philadelphia was 9-3)
4: 7 starts (Philadelphia was 4-3)
5+: 11 starts (Philadelphia was 2-9)
```

As long as he didn't get lit up, it didn't really
matter how well Alexander pitched. His team won the
majority of his starts regardless of how many runs he
allowed. Despite that, Alexander set shutout records,
guaranteeing his team a perfect record in those games.

- Jack Nabors finished the 1916 season with a 3.47 ERA and a record of 1-20. Yes, a 3.47 ERA was above the league average of 2.72, but certainly not 1-20 bad. Nabors' only win in 1916 came when he tossed a complete game and allowed no earned runs (and two unearned). He's the only player in MLB history with twenty losses and no more than a single victory in a season. From April 28 until the end of the season, Nabors went 0-19 in 36 games (27 starts) with a 3.68 ERA.

- On May 9, the Athletics and Tigers set a nine inning MLB record by walking a total of 30 times in the game. Philadelphia went 3-for-28 at the plate with 12 walks. Who started that game for the A's? None other than Jack Nabors, who allowed three walks and five runs in his only inning of work. He was succeeded by Harry Weaver, who walked three in his one inning, who was then followed by Carl Ray, who allowed twelve walks in his seven inning relief appearance. Bernie Boland, a pitcher for Detroit, became the only relief pitcher since at least 1908 with a hit and three walks in a game. Detroit's starter, George Cunningham, went one-for-one with a double and a walk. From their pitchers, the Tigers got a two-for-two game with four walks, a double, and two runs batted in.

- The Giants set an MLB record with a 26 game unbeaten streak. Starting September 7, they won twelve games in a row, tied a game which was restarted the next day (which they won), and then won 12 more in a row for a total of 25 wins. The team also had a 17 game winning streak; after starting off 2-13, they managed to reach a 19-13 record. Their record streak brought them from 60-62 to 85-62.

Grover Cleveland Alexander's shutout record also netted him his second consecutive Triple Crown. Meanwhile, the New York Giants had possibly the streakiest season of all time, while Jack Nabors had perhaps the unluckiest.

1917

In their first World Series appearance since their 1906 win over the 116-win Cubs, the 100-54 White Sox, led by pitcher Eddie Cicotte, won their second ever World Series title. This time, their win came at the hands of the 98-56 New York Giants in six games. The White Sox would not win another World Series title until 2005. Meanwhile, with the United States in the midst of joining the Great War, Braves catcher Hank Gowdy became the first MLB player to enlist in the military during World War I. Gowdy missed the rest of the 1917 season and all of the 1918 season serving. He would return in 1919 and play until 1930. He'd later serve as a captain in World War II, and is believed to be the only MLB player to serve the United States in both World Wars. 1917 was also the first season in which earned run statistics were kept; all ER and ERA stats before 1917 have been retroactively calculated by historians.

Hall of Famers Lou Boudreau and Phil Rizzuto were born in 1917. Boudreau would play most of his career with Cleveland, where he led the AL with 45 doubles in three different seasons. Rizzuto would be the Yankees shortstop for seven of their World Series titles; he totaled 40.8 WAR in his thirteen seasons.

Ross Youngs made his debut in 1917. He would tragically have his career and life cut short due to a kidney disorder. In his ten seasons for the Giants, he racked up 1,491 hits and appeared in the World Series in four consecutive seasons, winning two championships.

Like 1916, many notable players played their final game in 1917. Eight time batting champion Honus Wagner ended his 21 year career with 3,420 hits and 723 stolen bases. Wagner is widely considered to be the greatest shortstop of all time. All-time triples leader Sam Crawford retired with 309 to his name; 1917 was his only triple-less season in his career. Ed Walsh, baseball's all-time ERA leader at 1.82, pitched in his final game of his fourteen season career. His first thirteen seasons came with the White Sox, but he was not part of their 1917 championship squad. Eddie Plank also retired following 1917; he's the only pitcher in MLB history with a dozen wins in each of his first fifteen seasons, and owns career complete game (410) and shutout (69) records for left-handed pitchers.

Interesting numbers from the 1917 season:
- Ty Cobb recorded his second career season with at least 150 singles, 70 extra base hits, and 50 stolen bases. Everyone else who has ever played in the Majors has combined for zero such seasons.
- Cobb's 1917 season, by Wins Above Replacement, was the best of his career, at 11.3. He owns each of the top five seasons (and three other seasons in the top 25) in terms of WAR by a position player in Tigers history.
- Cobb's 1917 is also the most recent instance in MLB history in which a player led the Majors in both stolen bases and extra base hits. With his 55 stolen bases, Cobb became the

first player in American League history to lead the league in stolen bases for three consecutive years.

- Over his 35 game hitting streak from May 31 to July 7, Cobb batted .464/.516/.754 with 25 extra base hits and thirteen stolen bases. His 162 game pace over that span? 297 hits, 61 doubles, 42 triples, fourteen home runs, and 61 stolen bases!
- Red Sox second baseman Jack Barry laid down 54 sacrifice hits, the third most in a season in MLB history. However, it wasn't even enough to lead his league, as Cleveland shortstop Ray Chapman set a still-standing record with 67 sacrifices.
- Gavvy Cravath became the first player in MLB history with six consecutive seasons of double-digit home runs. No other active player had more than four such seasons in their entire career.
- Giants shortstop Art Fletcher became the second player in MLB history with 5+ defensive WAR in a season, joining Terry Turner's 1906 season. Since, Andrelton Simmons and Kevin Kiermaier have joined the 5 dWAR club. Fletcher also led the National League in hit by pitches for the fourth time in five seasons.
- Tigers shortstop Donie Bush's 112 runs scored led baseball. It was Bush's seventh season with at least 95 runs scored, the third most in Tigers history behind only Ty Cobb and Charlie Gehringer. Bush is also one of only four shortstops with at least seven such seasons before turning 30 (also Álex Rodríguez, Derek Jeter, and Herman Long).
- Pete Alexander won a major league best 30 games for the Phillies in 1917. It was his fourth straight season leading the National League in wins, only Warren Spahn has had a longer streak (1957-1961) in his career. It was also his third consecutive season leading MLB in wins, only Robin Roberts

would have a longer such stretch (1952-1955) in his career.

- Walter Johnson recorded his third consecutive season with a FIP under 2.00. Clayton Kershaw is the only pitcher since to manage even back-to-back such seasons. It would've been five consecutive seasons for Johnson if his 1914 FIP was a few points lower. (He finished at 1.90 in 1913 and 2.02 in 1914.)
- On June 23, Babe Ruth was ejected from his start after walking the leadoff batter. Ernie Shore came in to relieve Ruth. The leadoff hitter was caught stealing second base, and Shore retired the next 26 hitters in order. Shore was credited with a perfect game, but since then, the rules for a perfect game have been changed and Shore no longer gets credit for the perfect game. Ruth and Shore are still considered to have thrown a combined no-hitter.
- Burleigh Grimes finished his rookie season with three wins and sixteen losses; that's a Win-Loss% of .158! Out of the 973 seasons in which a Hall of Fame pitcher had at least 15 decisions, Grimes' 1917 season is the worst of them all in terms of winning percentage.
- Indians pitcher Stan Coveleski led all of baseball with nine shutouts on the season and his teammate Jim Bagby would finish the season tied for the second most with eight, along with Pete Alexander of the Phillies and Walter Johnson of the Senators. Coveleski and Bagby are one of just two duos to post eight or more shutouts in the same season, Mordecai Brown and Orval Overall accomplished this same feat for the Chicago Cubs in 1909. When you consider that there were only nineteen complete game shutouts thrown in the Major Leagues in 2018 and no more than one for any pitcher, it's pretty safe to say that this will never happen again.

1917 saw the continued dominance of the league's stars, including Ty Cobb, Pete Alexander, and Walter Johnson. Meanwhile, several other former stars closed out their careers with the 1917 season. The South Side of Chicago saw what would be its last World Series victory for nearly 90 seasons.

1918

With World War I factoring into a shortened Major League schedule, the Chicago Cubs would finish the season with an 84-45 record on their way to winning the National League by ten and a half games over the defending NL champion New York Giants. In the American League, the Boston Red Sox would climb back to the top of the standings with a record of 75-51 and finishing two and a half games ahead of the Cleveland Indians. Boston would go on to beat the Cubs four games to two in the low-scoring World Series, despite being outscored ten to nine in the six game Series. It's the third championship in four seasons for the Red Sox and their fifth title in the fifteen years that there has been a non-exhibition World Series.

Ted Williams, Bob Feller, Pee Wee Reese, and Bobby Doerr were all born in 1918. Williams' .482 career on-base percentage is the best of all time. Feller led the American League in wins six times, on his way to winning 266 career games with a 3.25 ERA, all with Cleveland. Reese, a career Dodger shortstop, totaled 66.3 WAR in his career, while Red Sox second baseman Bobby Doerr was worth 51.2. All four of these Hall of Fame greats would trade in their baseball uniforms for military uniforms during World War II.

Jake Beckley, a twenty-year veteran of the game, would pass away at the age of 50. At the time of Beckley's retirement in 1907, he was the all-time leader in triples with 244; only Sam Crawford, Ty Cobb, and Honus Wagner finished their careers with more three-base hits.

Waite Hoyt would make his Majors debut in 1918 with the New York Giants, striking out two in a clean inning of work; he'd then quit the organization and go play semi-pro baseball when the Giants demoted him back to the minors shortly after his first big league appearance. He'd return to the Majors with the Red Sox in 1919. Also making his MLB debut was Jesse Haines. Haines and Hoyt would pester hitters for the next two decades on their way to careers worthy of Cooperstown.

Bobby Wallace's career would come to an end after 25 big league seasons. He'd began his career as a pitcher, was moved to the outfield, and then spent a couple seasons playing third base before he found the position that landed him the nickname "Mr. Shortstop." Wallace would accumulate 76.3 WAR during his Hall of Fame career. Also playing in the last game of his career was Hughie Jennings. The 49-year-old Jennings made his final appearance on September 2nd as a defensive substitute at first base, it was his first game in over six years and just his sixth appearance in the past fifteen years. Those final six games of Jennings' career were all with the Detroit Tigers and all with him being the manager of the team.

Interesting numbers from the 1918 season:
- There were no home runs hit in the 1918 World Series; this was the fourth time that has ever happened (1905, 1906, 1907).

A century has since passed, but the 1918 World Series is still the most recent World Series without a home run.

- Heinie Groh led baseball with 86 runs scored. It was the first time that no player scored 100 runs in a season since 1882, when George Gore's 99 earned him the run title. It'd be another 50 years until the sport's leader failed to score 100, when Glenn Beckert's 98 was enough to lead baseball in 1968.

- Zack Wheat of the Brooklyn Robins would end the season strong with a .335 batting average, good enough to edge out Edd Roush for the National League batting title. Wheat remains the only player to ever win a batting title without hitting a home run that year.

- Gavvy Cravath's streak of seasons with double-digit home runs ended, but he still led the National League with eight homers. However, he only slashed .232/.320/.376, a relatively average line (106 OPS+) given the time period.

- The 1918 season marked a couple of lasts in baseball history with regard to home runs. It was the last year in which no players hit 20+ homers and the last time a team failed to hit five home runs in a season. Yes, you read that right. An entire team couldn't hit a total of five roundtrippers in 1918. That team was the Washington Senators and, in fact, the season before those same Senators only hit four. Those two teams plus the 1908 and 1909 Chicago White Sox are the only teams without five home runs in a season since the mound was moved back to its current distance of 60 feet 6 inches in 1893.

- Babe Ruth's eleven home runs was tied for the most in baseball; it's the first of twelve times he would lead the American League in home runs. Ruth's .555 SLG and .966 OPS led the American League; he'd lead the AL in both of these categories another dozen times apiece throughout his career. As if it wasn't enough to be leading the league in all three of those offensive statistics, Ruth also finished top ten in the American League in ERA, WHIP, W-L%, ERA+, and complete games in 1918!

- On April 19th, the Boston Red Sox defeated the New York Yankees by a score of 9-5. Babe Ruth picked up the complete game victory on the mound for the Red Sox that day. This gave Ruth his ninth winning decision over the Yankees in his past nine games against them. Since 1908, Babe is the only pitcher to get credited with a win in nine consecutive appearances against the Yankees.

- With his home run on May 7, Babe Ruth became the first player in nearly half of a decade to hit an over-the-fence home run against Walter Johnson. Just over a month later, Ruth took Johnson deep again. After that, it'd be nearly two more years until someone would hit one over the fence off Johnson. It was Ruth again, obviously.

- For the second time in his career, Walter Johnson had earned the American League's Triple Crown for Pitching. He led all of the Majors with 23 wins, a 1.27 ERA, and 162 strikeouts. At the time, Johnson joined Christy Mathewson and Grover Cleveland Alexander as the only pitchers to win the Pitching Triple Crown twice, and he was the first to win it twice in the American League.

- Walter Johnson wasn't the only pitcher to win the Triple Crown in 1918. Hippo Vaughn of the Chicago Cubs would attain that honor in the National League as well; he put up 22 wins, a 1.74 ERA, and 148 strikeouts to lead the senior circuit.

- Hippo Vaughn (1.74 ERA) and Lefty Tyler (2.00 ERA) of the Chicago Cubs made National League history when they became the only set of left-handed teammates to post a 2.00 ERA or lower in the same season.

- On August 1st, the Pittsburgh Pirates and the Boston Braves played 20 innings of score-free baseball before Pittsburgh put up two runs in the top of the 21st inning on their way to a 2-0 victory. Art Nehf would pitch all 21 innings for the Braves that day on his way to being credited with the loss.
- Red Sox pitchers tossed 25 complete game shutouts in 1918. It's the last time an American League team would reach that mark. Only the 1944 Cardinals and the 1968 Cardinals would ever put up that many complete game shutouts in a season that wasn't during the Dead Ball Era.

The 1918 season gave us a glimpse of what Babe Ruth was, a hitter that could pitch, and not the other way around. Baseball also saw the Pitching Triple Crown accomplished in both leagues for the first time since 1905. The Boston Red Sox continued their early dominance of the American League by winning their sixth pennant and defeating the National League in the World Series for the fifth time in five tries, but their reign at the top would come to an abrupt halt. The Red Sox would have to wait 28 more years to win another AL pennant and 86 more years to win another World Series.

1919

Under the newly constructed 140-game schedule the Cincinnati Reds led baseball with 96 regular season wins. Their World Series opponents, the Chicago White Sox, won an AL-best 88 games. The 1919 season was not without controversy, however. Eight members of the Chicago "Black Sox" were accused of throwing the Series for money from a gambling group headed by Arnold Rothstein. The players would be permanently banned from professional baseball, as well as honors that include enshrinement in the Baseball Hall of Fame. Many argue that the most notable player on the team, Shoeless Joe Jackson, should have a plaque in Cooperstown, as he batted .375/.394/.563 in the Series and was the only player on either team with a dozen hits. His 0.58 WPA was also the second best of all players in the 1919 World Series, and he failed to commit any errors in the field. In the end, the Reds won the World Series five games to three.

Jackie Robinson and Monte Irvin, two of MLB's earliest African American players, were born in the early months of 1919. Robinson, one of baseball's most underrated players, had a .311/.409/.474 slash line in his career while averaging around 150 hits, 45 extra base hits, 20 steals, and over 6.0 WAR per season. Irvin unfortunately did not play in the Majors until he was 30, but he led the NL in RBI in 1951.

Jim O'Rourke, most known for being baseball's all-time home run leader following the 1882 season, died at 68. O'Rourke is also the only Yale attendee to eclipse the 1,000 career hit mark.

Frankie Frisch and George Uhle made their debuts in 1919. Frisch would go on to win three stolen base titles in the National League, while Uhle would finish his career with exactly 200 victories.

Sherry Magee, the NL's best hitter in 1910 and collector of over 2,000 career hits, retired after the 1919 season. He capped off his career with a pinch hit single in Game 7 of the World Series for his would-be champion Reds.

Interesting numbers from the 1919 season:
- With his 166 OPS+ in 1919, Ty Cobb extended his record by becoming the only player in MLB history with thirteen consecutive seasons of a 165 OPS+ or better. The only other player to do it in ten consecutive seasons is Lou Gehrig (eleven in a row). In the thirteen seasons from 1907-1919, Cobb had a 188 OPS+.
- Babe Ruth broke Ned Williamson's 35-year-old record by hitting 29 home runs, despite the shortened schedule. The rest of Ruth's Red Sox combined for four home runs. His 29 homers were more than ten teams, or eleven if you include the rest of his Sox. Set on September 24, 1919, this single-season home run record would last for 299 days; he'd break his own record on July 19 of the following season.
- Ruth accounted for 6.4% of the home runs hit in the Majors in 1919 despite taking only 0.6% of the plate appearances.
- In his final pitching appearance for the Boston Red Sox, Babe

Ruth tossed 5.1 innings of three run ball. He was moved to left field, where he would break the 3-3 tie with a walk-off home run in the bottom of the ninth inning.

- 1919 would be the last season until 1945 (when many players were serving in World War II) in which no player reached the 30 home run threshold.

- With his dinger in the final game of the tainted World Series, Shoeless Joe Jackson owns the only ever home run that was hit in a World Series Game 8.

- Walter Johnson led the American League in strikeouts for the eighth consecutive season (his streak ended after 1919). He's the only pitcher in MLB history to lead his league in strikeouts for eight seasons in a row. Johnson averaged a little more than 212 strikeouts per season during that stretch. The great Cy Young never struck out more than 210 in any of his 21 big league seasons.

- 1919 was also Walter Johnson's third season with at least 140 strikeouts and no home runs allowed. No other pitcher in MLB history has put up multiple such seasons in their career.

- Johnson (290.1 IP) and Phil Douglas (213.0 IP) are the two most recent pitchers with 200 innings pitched and zero home runs allowed. From 2000 through 2018 (the writing of this book) the pitcher with the most innings pitched in a season without allowing a home run is Peter Moylan, who tossed 73.0 innings for the Atlanta Braves in 2009 without giving up a single long ball.

- In an odd coincidence, there was a three-way tie for most innings pitched in the 1919 season. Eddie Cicotte, Jim Shaw, and Hippo Vaughn each tossed exactly 306.2 innings. The next highest three-way tie for innings pitched in 1919 was 15.0 innings; actually four pitchers threw exactly 15.0 innings tying for 145th most that season.

- On July 7th, John Cavanaugh went 0-for-1 with a strikeout in his only career MLB game. In that seemingly inconsequential at bat, Cavanaugh became the first player born in the 1900s to play Major League Baseball.

Most known for the Black Sox scandal, 1919 also acted as a transition year from the Dead Ball Era to the Live Ball Era. Babe Ruth dominated headlines from season's start to year's end, as in the single most consequential transaction in baseball history, the Red Sox agreed to sell Ruth to the New York Yankees on December 26. The deal would not actually be announced until the first week of 1920, however.

* * *

Made in the USA
Coppell, TX
01 June 2021